Taking Charge of Your Spiritual Path
Nelle Moffett with Richard D. Bowers

For both those who have found a spiritual home and for those who are still looking, there is a need for spiritual seekers to have a better understanding of the process and principles of spiritual development. If you want to do practices that have meaning for you and to be able to change your practice when something more or different is needed, this book will provide you with some basic principles to help you take charge of your own spiritual path. People are taking more responsibility for managing their own finances, their own psychological wellbeing, and their own education. Likewise, it is possible now to take charge of one's own spiritual path. In most spiritual paths, the outcomes are often not made clear and the focus is placed on the practice itself without making the objective of the practice clear. This is disempowering for you, the practitioner. But now, we no longer have to stay stuck in this model. The purpose of this book is to identify some common underlying objectives of true spiritual practices outside of the doctrine that surrounds them. This book discusses the specific outcomes that different practices are designed to accomplish.

Taking Charge of Your Spiritual Path

Other Books by Nelle Moffett and Richard D. Bowers

Happiness is a Good Story: Finding Meaning in Life's Experiences

Empathy in Conflict Intervention: The Key to Successful NVC Mediation

Taking Charge of Your Spiritual Path

Nelle Moffett
with Richard D. Bowers

Harmony World Publishing
Jerome, AZ

**Copyright © 2016
by Nelle Moffett and Richard D. Bowers.** All rights reserved. No part of this book may be reproduced or utilized in any form or by any means, electronic or mechanical, including photocopying, recording, or by any information storage and retrieval system, without permission in writing from the publisher.

Cover photograph by Nelle Moffett.

Harmony World Publishing
PO Box 876
Jerome, AZ 86331-0876
www.harmonyworld.net

Printed in the United States of America

Trademarks: Nonviolent Communication, NVC, and The Center for Nonviolent Communication are trademarks of The Center for Nonviolent Communication located at 5600 San Francisco Rd. NE Suite A, Albuquerque, NM 87109.

Emotional Freedom Techniques is a registered service mark of Gary H. Craig located at P.O. Box 1393, Gualala CA 95445.

Bio-Geometric Integration is a registered service mark of Susan M. Brown located at 25W330 Geneva Road, Carol Stream IL 60188.

Somatic Experiencing is a registered service mark of Peter Levine , Ph.D. located at P.O. Box 110, Lyons, CO 80540.

Second Edition

ISBN 978-0-9911117-3-2

ISBN 978-0-9911-1171-8 1st Edition 2013

With gratitude

to all my teachers

Table of Contents

	Preface	vii
Chapter 1	Taking Charge of Your Spiritual Path	1
Chapter 2	Getting Beyond Fear and Doubt	7
Chapter 3	Know Yourself	17
Chapter 4	Objectives of Spiritual Practices	25
Chapter 5	Thoughts about Spiritual Practices	53
Chapter 6	Finding Spiritual Fellowship	81
Chapter 7	When You Fall into a Hole	85
Chapter 8	Some Cautions	101
Chapter 9	Measuring Progress	109
	Resources	115
	About the Authors	157

Preface

This book is written by two authors, Nelle and Rick. We enjoy writing together and take on different roles in each book. We believe that using "I" rather than "we" is more personal and connecting with the reader. It is also much less awkward than shifting back and forth from "we" to "I" and creating ambiguity about which one of us is speaking. In this book, Nelle is the primary author using the word "I" to tell her stories from her perspective.

1

Taking Charge of Your Spiritual Path

Are you ready to develop your own attunement, intuition, and direct relationship with the divine source? Do you want to be empowered to take responsibility for your own spiritual practice? Do you want to do practices that have meaning and purpose for you and want to be able to change your practice when something more or different is needed?

For both those who have found a spiritual home and for those who are still looking, there is a need for spiritual seekers to have a better understanding of the process and principles of spiritual development. We live in a time when

2   Taking Charge of Your Spiritual Path

there is an abundance of books and religious institutions promoting alternative spiritual paths, each offering a different set of rituals, practices, and beliefs. This abundance of spiritual paths, as well as variations in teachings within the same path, can be confusing. A friend of mine told me, "I am reading a lot of these spiritual gurus and find myself questioning everything."

The fastest growing religious category in the United States is "Spiritual but not religious." It appears to me that people who identify in this category still place a strong value on spirituality, but at the same time, are engaging in a process of redefining the form of expression for that spirituality. On the other hand, people who are following a spiritual path may want ways to deepen or better understand their practice.

Even if one is following a spiritual teacher, very often the teachings are provided in a general form (one-size-fits-all) or the advice given at one time appears to be in conflict with advice given at another time. In these cases, it still requires discrimination or "attunement" on the part of the disciples to apply the teachings to themselves. Whether you are following a spiritual teacher or not, it will likely become important at some point for you to take responsibility for your spiritual development.

These days, we are seeing the barrier breaking down between professionals and practitioners in many fields (e.g., medicine, education, psychotherapy). People are now taking more responsibility for becoming knowledgeable about their own health and taking charge of their diet, exercise, and supplements. People are taking more responsibility for managing their own finances, their own psychological

4   Taking Charge of Your Spiritual Path

wellbeing, and their own education. Likewise, it is possible now to take charge of one's own spiritual path. The knowledge of the spiritual processes and objectives is no longer held in secret by a small group of ordained and cloistered monks. Now, we no longer have to stay stuck in this old model, despite the fear-inducing messages that some religious teachers preach.

The purpose of this book is to identify some common underlying objectives of true spiritual practices outside of the doctrine that surrounds them and to open you to a range of spiritual practices from which you can select what fits for you. There actually are specific outcomes that different practices are designed to accomplish. In most spiritual paths, the outcomes are not made clear and the focus is placed on the practice itself without making the objective of the practice clear. This is disempowering for the practitioner.

A practice is not in itself sacred. There is nothing sacred about chanting or meditation or prayer in themselves. Performing these practices without understanding what they are designed to accomplish has some value but it is limited and we can go beyond this level of dependency.

In a specific path, the common pattern is to rely on the teacher or minister to understand these deeper purposes and to prescribe practices to the followers. But there is nothing sacred about this relationship either. A relationship with a spiritual teacher can be useful when the teacher is more advanced and understands the underlying principles (which are not always the case) and when followers do not want to or are not ready to take responsibility for developing this understanding for themselves in order to design their own practices.

My assumption in this book is that you are not content with a purely dependent relationship with a guru, minister, or teacher in spiritual matters and that you desire to take on the challenge and responsibility for your own spiritual practice. You may want to be able to have empowered conversations with your current spiritual guide about your practices and what they are for. You also want to develop your own attunement, intuition, and direct relationship with the divine source. In other words, you want to be empowered to take responsibility for your own spiritual practice. You want to do practices that have meaning and purpose for you and you want to be able to change your practice when something more or different is needed. This book will provide you with some basic principles to help you take charge of your own spiritual path.

2

Getting Beyond Fear and Doubt

Every spiritual seeker encounters fears and doubts on the spiritual path and needs to be prepared to work with them in a constructive way. If you have been brought up in a religion, you have most likely absorbed a lot of fear-based messages about sin and damnation if you leave your temple, church, synagogue, or mosque or stop doing the prescribed rituals and practices. You have most likely been taught that you must have an ordained spiritual teacher in order to be successful. You may have received alarming messages about the importance of loyalty to the one (true) path or else your soul will be lost. These messages, lodged in our subconscious minds, are lurking in wait to sabotage any move towards independent thinking.

If you are fortunate to have missed these messages somehow, you may have other thoughts about your own inadequacy, lack of sufficient knowledge, doubts about your ability to reach enlightenment, God, spirit, or other word you use to describe your spiritual goal. Perhaps you have an inkling of an evil power or subverting ego that will come up to thwart your efforts. People in your life or your own self-talk may be telling you that it is safer to stay in a church, mosque, temple, or synagogue even if it is not fulfilling to you than to launch out on your own.

To overcome these obstacles of fear and doubt, I believe it is important to have a framework of belief that you can rely on. If you do not have such a framework that is strongly rooted <u>within yourself</u>, it may in fact be better for you to stay in a church, temple, mosque, or synagogue that comes closest to your beliefs and from which you can have support for your spiritual practices. On the other hand, if you can identify a framework of belief for yourself that can sustain you when thoughts of fearful punishment and inadequacy arise, then you have a foundation for being your own spiritual guide.

When I talk about a "framework of belief," I do not mean finding the right belief system, or finding the Truth. As human beings, by definition, we will always have a partial view until we become enlightened. In the meantime, we need a "place to stand" recognizing that this will likely change as we get more experience on the spiritual path.

10   Taking Charge of Your Spiritual Path

We can have a place to stand and at the same time be flexible and allow it to develop as our understanding changes and develops. In any given moment, we can stand within the best framework of belief that we are capable of articulating and be willing to revise it according to our own inner guidance.

I have a framework of belief that is meaningful to me and sustains me. I find the basis for this framework within many spiritual paths and so it occurs to me that there is broad support and validation for this framework. At the same time, I recognize that this is only a partial statement of the principles that guide me and that this framework will likely change as my perspective changes.

I will share it with you here as an example of what you might put together for yourself. You might even want to create something like this as your own Creed or Statement of Faith.

Nelle's Creed

I believe:

1. God is Love.
2. I am created in the image of God, therefore my true Self is Love.
3. I am not separate nor have I ever been separate from God.
4. I already am all that I seek to be; there is nothing to achieve on the spiritual path.
5. All that is needed is for me to realize this Truth.

What this Creed provides for me is the assurance I need when fears and doubts arise. From this framework, I can see how silly it is for me to be afraid that, if I launch out on my own or stop meditating or miss a practice, I will be condemned or shut out from God in some way.

- How can using the "right" or "wrong" meditation posture or technique keep me from the love of God? Preposterous!

- How can any perceived lack in me put my relationship with God in jeopardy? Never! Nothing that I do or fail to do will make God love me more or less. God's love is unconditional and cannot be earned or lost.

- How can my ego's sabotaging messages get between me and God? Childish fears! Imagined monsters under the bed can never hurt me.

A story about my own experience may illustrate how I used my foundational beliefs to deal with a spiritual challenge. After I had been meditating dutifully for 20 years morning and night, I came to the realization that I was still miserable. Meditation didn't really support me in the way I thought it should. Upon reflection over a period of time, I realized that my meditation practice was coming entirely from fear and wanting to please God and Guru. I thought that if I was a "good girl" then I would be accepted and loved by God and then I would be happy.

When I saw this clearly in myself, I knew that this was not the basis of a healthy spiritual practice. This was an old belief system that I was still carrying in me. I knew intuitively that I needed to stop meditating to shift this energy. But Wow! That was a very scary thought. I wrestled with my fear for a while before I mustered the courage to take the plunge and stop meditating. The courage came from my deeper belief that God is Love and that nothing

14 Taking Charge of Your Spiritual Path

I did or didn't do would change God's Love for me. But I had to put it to the test by stopping my meditation practice. I did stop meditating, and I didn't die!

It was some years later that I was able to start a meditation practice again. I was able to restart my meditation practice from a different perspective, from an inner desire to meditate, to look forward to meditating and enjoy it rather than doing it from a perspective of duty or obligation. Meditating from this empowered perspective provides me with a much more positive experience.

By empowering myself to take charge of my spiritual path, I have been able to shift my focus from "doing things right" to generating the inner peace, joy, and love that I seek. Instead of forcing myself into a shoe that doesn't fit, I am finding joy and contentment through self-acceptance and nurturing the presence of God that is already within. What I want to share with you in this book is some of the wisdom that I have received in my own journey.

3

Know Yourself

There are potentially thousands of possible spiritual practices. It is not possible nor is it required to do them all. Even within one spiritual path, there are potentially more practices than any one person can or should do. If you have a Type A personality (over-the-top, extreme achievement oriented), it is important to remind yourself that doing more is not necessarily better. So how do you determine which practices and how many practices are beneficial for you? Here is one place to start.

Hindu philosophy identifies three spiritual styles: action-oriented, devotion-oriented, and wisdom-oriented. There are also three different levels of spiritual energy: low, active, and uplifted. It may be helpful for you to identify your style and energy level to help sort through the spiritual practices and select those that fit you. If you pick practices that fit your style and energy level you will find more ease and contentment in your practice. Type A's pay attention here. You do not necessarily go faster, achieve more, or gain more spiritual points by struggling and working harder.

Action-Oriented Style

A person with this style thrives through service to others, through doing good works, and through physical practices. Some examples of action-oriented practices, if done for the purpose of worshipping or keeping mindful of Spirit, are walking a Labyrinth, volunteering, hatha yoga, Chi Qong, chanting, Sufi dancing, gardening, cooking. There is a community in India where the women have a daily spiritual practice of bathing, dressing, and feeding a baby-doll Krishna as an example of an action-based practice. Theoretically, any action can be done with the consciousness of worship.

Devotion-Oriented Style

A person with this style thrives through expressing love for the divine. Some examples of devotion-oriented practices are chanting, compassion meditation, communing with the divine, relating to spirit as the Beloved, repeating the name of the Beloved, ecstatic meditation, monasticism (being married to God), serving the divine through one's spouse, constantly thinking of the Beloved, heart-based meditation, writing poetry to the Beloved, merging oneself with the Beloved.

Wisdom-Oriented Style

A person with this style thrives through practices that apply the mind and discrimination. Some examples of wisdom-oriented practices are reading uplifting books, studying the lives of saints, studying and applying different spiritual paths, studying spiritual texts, practicing "neti-neti" (not this, not that), cognitive affirmations, recognizing the illusion, watching the mind, naming the thoughts, watching identifications (who am I).

Low Energy

Do you ever have a case of the blues or pervasive "I don't want to" feelings? These are examples of low energy. Low energy may be sluggish or even depressed. You may find that your usual physical and mental resources are not available to you. Doubt and self-criticism may be stealthily or blatantly present. Negative thoughts and perceptions are most prevalent and your spiritual aspirations may be hard to find. When low energy is dominant, you may want to engage yourself in energizing and uplifting practices.

Active Energy

Productivity, busy-ness, and outward focus are characteristics of this type of energy. You have abundant energy and drive to get things done and are usually effective and efficient in the process. Your mind is sharp, thinking ahead, and full of creative thoughts. Your body is throbbing with energy and it is hard to sit still. When active energy is dominant, you may want to balance with some practices that are relaxing and uplifting.

Uplifting Energy

This energy tends to be more inward and expansive. It is easy to connect with compassion for yourself and others. You may feel yourself as larger than your body and connected with all of creation. Your mind is quiet and peaceful and your heart is open. Forgiveness flows naturally. You are able to stay connected with this expansive energy even while you are engaged in outward activities. You are able to stay even-minded in the circumstances that might otherwise annoy you. When uplifting energy is dominant, you may want to balance with some practices that are grounding and energizing if you have a tendency toward spaciness.

How to Use Personality and Energy Typing

A caution about personality and energy typing is important to recognize. Human beings are complex and reflect the whole of creation. We all have all of the types and all of the energy levels in us. At the same time, like snowflakes and finger prints, we have our unique combinations of characteristics. While you may have a clear dominant style and energy level, you will likely recognize that you have more than one of these styles and that you have each of the energy levels at different times.

This is perfect, because you can see how difficult it is to have a one-size-fits-all spiritual practice! You may need to have a set of practices when your energy and inclinations swing in one direction and another set when your energy and style shift in another direction.

Since you have inside information and can sense what you need in any given time, you can adjust your practices accordingly. As you read the rest of this book and as you look for practices in other sources, you can keep your spiritual style and energy level in mind. With this information, you are empowered to design your practices according to your shifting needs.

4

Objectives of Spiritual Practices

Spiritual practices are tools to help us develop specific awareness and energy. Different practices achieve different ends. Each practice is like a finger pointing to an outcome. The point of the practice is to look at the outcome rather than the finger. Here is a list of some of the universal outcomes or objectives of spiritual practice.

1. Moving the energy in a positive (upward) direction

2. Quieting the mind of the noise of self-talk

3. Cultivating the Inner Witness

4. Shifting from fear to love
5. Cultivating inner peace, joy, and love
6. Being aware of and expanding our identification
7. Changing our perception of this world from separation to unity

Intellectual understanding of these objectives is not enough. What we want is to have an actual experience of the effects of these objectives. I believe this is most often accomplished through practices. Practices are actions that we do regularly and repeatedly. We are practicing ways of being, thinking, and taking action that will produce specific effects eventually, over time. Practicing means that we have not yet perfected these ways of being and it takes repetition and regularity to create mastery in each of these outcomes.

Objectives of Spiritual Practices

This may sound contradictory to what I said earlier, that there is nothing to achieve on the spiritual path. In my belief system, there is nothing to achieve because we already are and already have everything that we desire. The only problem is that we don't see it, believe it, and experience this fullness of "already-beingness."

Rather than adding something to us that is somehow missing, these practices help to remove the barriers to our perception. Have you ever had the experience of not seeing something that someone else is pointing to and then, all of a sudden, you see it? In this instance, are you any different than you were before? Any better? Any smarter? Any wiser? Probably not. First you couldn't see it, and then you did. Spiritual enlightenment is something like that. Through practice, we begin to perceive things differently. What was previously invisible to us becomes clear, sometimes gradually, but often in a sudden flash of new insight.

There is a story about a frog that fell into a pail of milk. The frog could not get out of the pail, so all it could do was to swim and swim and swim. It started to get tired, but just kept on swimming. When it became so tired it couldn't swim any more, it suddenly felt this ball underneath it that was keeping it afloat. All of the swimming had churned the milk into butter! We can consider our practices like the frog swimming in the pail of milk; our swimming will eventually create spiritual butter. So now let's look in more detail at each of the universal spiritual objectives that I listed above, as a place to start.

Moving the Energy in a Positive (Upward) Direction

This objective contains two parts: direction and flow. Energy is either moving toward Spirit or enlightenment or away from Spirit or enlightenment. The spiritual path is "directional." For some people, the first step is an "About-Face." Conversion experiences often accomplish this reversal of direction.

The directional nature of the spiritual path is one reason that spiritual advice may seem contradictory. The spiritual journey is often experienced as a continuum toward a goal, or committed practice in the same direction. In this analogy, what a person needs for their next step depends on where they are along the journey. For example, for one person, their next step forward may be to get a job and become financially responsible. For another person, their next step forward may be to quit their job and become a renunciant. One person may need to strengthen their ego and another person may need to become less attached to the ego.

When we hear stories of saints and the practices they have undertaken, it does not follow that these practices are right for us and that we should be able to do the same things. Our spiritual development is not served by setting up unrealistic goals for ourselves. The key here is to know where you stand and to discern your next small step forward.

The second part of this objective is flow or movement. It is not just the direction we are facing that is important, but we also need to be in motion. When we are in motion, we can more easily steer our course. A sailboat without any wind cannot make progress even if it is pointed in the right direction.

Sometimes, the hardest step is from inaction to action. It is important to stimulate our energy in order to put wind in our sails. Often when we are stuck in place, we are making some unrealistic demand on our self for the next step. If you are having trouble getting into action, it is sometimes helpful to identify a next step that would be so ridiculously easy to do that you will have no trouble doing it.

It is important to do something to get yourself in motion, no matter how small or insignificant that step may seem. I would even say that it is more important to be in motion than to be facing in the right direction. When we are not in motion, the direction we are facing has little consequence. Once we are in motion, we can be guided in the right direction. It is like my GPS says, "Move to the highlighted route and then the route guidance will begin."

Quieting the Mind of the Noise of Self-talk

If you haven't already tried some form of meditation, you may not realize how noisy your mind is. After about age seven, our minds are constantly busy with self-talk, commentary, judgments, planning, complaining, advice giving, story-telling and other noisy activities. The mind constantly generates this chatter even if you are not consciously listening to it. The purpose of many meditation practices is to start to quiet this chatter and to gain some amount of awareness of one's thoughts.

Why is quieting the mind important on the spiritual path? There are many reasons and benefits of quieting the mind. First of all, notice that I said "quieting" and not "silencing." The mind does what the mind does and this will not likely stop. But we can slow it down and become more aware of what the mind is saying and even begin to have greater choice about what the mind focuses on.

Awareness of the noise is the first step and can feel quite overwhelming when you first encounter it. The second step, through continued practice, is to begin to hear (become aware of) what the mind is saying. What the mind is saying to us underneath our awareness actually has significant power over our choices in life.

When we become more aware of what the mind is saying, we can understand why we do some of the things we do. From this awareness we can begin to empower ourselves to direct the mind toward what we want to create rather than being an unwitting victim of our unconscious thoughts. It is in this choice with our own thoughts that we can gain some empowerment on the spiritual path.

When we can begin to turn the mind in the spiritual direction and use the mind to support our intentions we gain a significant momentum on the spiritual path. With awareness of what the mind is saying, we can begin to use discrimination and realize that we do not have to believe everything the mind is telling us.

The mind replays many messages that are inherited from bad experiences in the past, including messages that tell us how bad or inadequate we are. One person I know said, "If we treated our friends the way we treat ourselves, we wouldn't have any friends." Much of our self-talk may be harsh and critical messages about our self that are simply false. When these thoughts go unexamined and unchallenged, we behave as if they are true.

Shifting from believing everything our minds tells us to questioning and doubting and challenging these thoughts is one aspect of directional positioning mentioned above. In order to choose whether to believe or disbelieve our thoughts, we first have to be able to hear them. Quieting the mind through meditation or contemplative practices allows the space and awareness to be able to catch our thoughts before they fly by unheard.

Cultivating the Inner Witness

Some meditations, as well as other types of inner awareness or contemplative practices, help to cultivate what is called an Inner Witness. What is meant by an Inner Witness is the ability to step back from our thoughts and observe them without getting caught up in them. This is a big step on the spiritual path, when we realize that we are not our thoughts. We become more able to disentangle and separate ourselves from our thoughts and simply watch them.

Cultivating the Inner Witness means creating some distance or space between our thoughts and our self. The witness is able to examine the thoughts, evaluate them, and choose whether to believe them and act on them or not. Cultivating the Inner Witness has the effect of reducing our reactivity, or automatic reactions to circumstances.

But who is watching the thoughts? When we are able to observe our thoughts, then we are able to identify our self with the Inner Witness rather than with the thoughts themselves. Identification with the Inner Witness helps us to disentangle our attachment and absorption in the drama of our minds and instead to be able to choose where we focus our attention. This step is critical in developing inner freedom and shifting the focus of our identification, which is discussed more later on.

Shifting from Fear to Love

Shifting from fear to love may be the biggest directional issue we face on the spiritual path. Fear keeps us small. Fear produces anxiety, defensiveness, and attack. Fear feeds our doubts, judgments, and sense of urgency. Fear has us try to prove something. Fear has us stop questioning. Fear keeps us dependent and subservient. Fear keeps us looking at the darkness and expecting the worst. Fear keeps us entangled in the drama. There is nothing uplifting about fear. Fear of God cripples our spiritual aspirations and keeps us focused on doing good and looking good for all the wrong reasons. Fear keeps us identified with the ego and the body.

If God is love, as most religions profess, and we are made in God's image, then love is our true nature. When we cultivate love, we connect with uplifting energy. Love is the opposite of fear. Love is expansive. Love creates more love. Love connects us to our highest expression. Love empowers us to step into our highest self. Love needs no defenses. Love includes others. Love allows us to approach God as a welcoming and unconditionally accepting Father, Mother, Friend or Beloved. Love has us turn and face the Light and expect the best. Love unites us with all of creation. Love breaks the hold of the ego and opens the door to identification with our higher Self, with Spirit.

I am describing the effects of fear and love from the standpoint of consciousness on the spiritual path. It is important also to recognize that some messages of fear are there to alert us to physical or emotional danger. These messages are important to attend to by making healthy, empowered choices regarding our safety. We can take appropriate action out of love for ourselves and not let our fear immobilize us into inaction, victimhood, or disempowered resignation.

The choice between fear and love is a primary basis of the spiritual path. We make this choice every moment without being aware that we are doing so. Spiritual practices that exercise this fear/love muscle might include the Buddhist practices of Loving-kindness or Tonglen, forgiveness practice, and empathy or perspective-taking practices. Two practices, Focusing and empathy through Nonviolent Communication™, teach how to listen with compassion to the parts of us that are afraid.

The more often we choose love, the stronger this muscle becomes. The more often we choose love, the more often we receive the experience of love. The more often we receive the experience of love, the more we want love. The more we experience and want love, the more often we will choose love.

Cultivating Inner Peace, Joy, and Love

Specific practices can help us to cultivate a state of being that contains the peace, joy, and love that we all are seeking. However, there are some misunderstandings in many seekers that may cause disillusionment on the spiritual path. First of all, neither meditation nor any other practice that I know of will produce instant peace, joy, and love. In fact, the seeker may seldom feel peace, joy or love during a spiritual practice.

There is an odd paradox that when we seek peace, for instance, then what we get is not peace but instead everything that stands in the way of our feeling peace. This makes sense when you remember that we are already the peace that we seek; all we have to do is see past all the things that create the appearance of disharmony in our minds and we will then see the reality of the peace that we already are.

This is a neat twist, but still can feel very frustrating when we do our practices and don't seem to be able to connect with the peace that we want. And then that same frustration gets in the way of our connection with inner peace! What a tangle this can be! The path to the qualities of peace, joy, and love is not instantaneous and may take us to some unexpected places. At the same time, the spiritual path is not about jumping into the deep end of the pool before we know how to swim.

One thing to be aware of is what you may be praying for and how that could show up in your life. At one point, I was enjoying the St. Francis prayer that says, 'Where there is hatred, let me sow Love; where there is darkness, Light" when I suddenly realized that I was praying to be put in places where there is darkness and hatred! I quickly altered my prayer to one that was more suited to my nature. I knew a monk who described a disciple who was praying "Lord, mold me according to Thy Design." The monk commented that this was a very brave disciple!

On the one hand, seeking peace, joy, and love can bring us face to face with the opposite qualities. On the other hand, we can choose to experience peace, joy, and love in the moment. Meher Baba, an Indian guru, is known for the phrase, "Don't worry; be happy." If your mind is like mine, you may reply, 'Well, that's easy for you to say!" So let's look at how that seemingly simplistic phrase really is expressing a deep spiritual truth.

There is a saying that worrying doesn't fry an egg. On a very practical level, worry doesn't get a task done any faster or better and in fact can get in the way of both. On a more esoteric level, if you believe that, as a soul, you already are everything you seek to be, then there is really nothing to worry about. All there is to do is just do what needs to be done, without the worry about the outcome. Just fry the egg without all the drama!

- If you believe that this world is a dream, then what is happening here isn't really happening and so there is nothing to worry about.

- If you believe that God is the creator and everything is in His/Her hands, then there is nothing to worry about.

- If you believe that God is everywhere present and all powerful, then there is nothing to worry about.

- If you believe that God is love, then there is nothing to worry about.

If you don't see your belief system reflected in the examples above, then add your version that can get you to a place of "nothing to worry about."

What about being happy? How can we just turn on happiness? If you believe that peace, joy, and love are yours by nature, then getting past what is in the way of those qualities will expose what is already there. If we let go of all the worrying about the outcome of our actions, then we create the space for our natural joy to bubble up. When we begin to trust the design of this universe instead of resisting it, we will feel the peace that is already there. If we look beyond our judgments of the circumstances around us to find the truth of underlying peace, joy, and love, then we will discover the source of happiness that is not dependent on circumstances to be just the way we wish them to be.

There is a saying, "Pain exists; suffering is optional." When you find yourself in suffering, this is an opportunity for self-compassion as well as using additional practices for reconnecting yourself with your spiritual truths about yourself and the world. I believe that access to being happy ultimately comes from this connection. Our practices will make it easier for us to reconnect when we notice that we are stuck in suffering. I will talk more about this process in a later chapter.

Being Aware of and Expanding our Identification

Several of the previous objectives have pointed to and prepared the ground for expansion of our identification. Currently, we are mostly identified with the body and personality. In fact, this is the definition that Paramhansa Yogananda, an Indian guru, gave for the ego; spirit identified with the body.

When we are able even occasionally to dis-identify from our thoughts, fears, worries, and circumstances we can begin to shift the focus of our identification towards something bigger. It may begin by stating our identity in the negative form, such as, "I am not the body, "I am not the ego," or "I am not a victim of my circumstances." I have found the following affirmation very useful in times of stress: "Praise does not make me any better than I am and blame does not make me any worse than I am."

Affirmations stated in the negative are not enough, however. To expand our sense of identification, we need to support our sense of connection with a bigger Self than the body, personality, and ego. In my belief system, the truth about me is that I am a child of God, created whole, perfect and complete. I am a spiritual being. I am unconditional love. I am without sin, as God is without sin. My practice includes daily lessons that remind me of my true nature and help me to notice when my identification has constricted to a little ego in a body.

There are clear signs when my identification has constricted such as worry, fear, judgment, attack of myself or others, urgency, emotional upset, sense of lack or something missing, or sense of separation from Source. *A Course in Miracles*, a Christian mystical text, says that any response to our life that is not joyful is a signal that helps us to recognize when we are identifying ourselves with a small, separate ego. Identification of our self as a separate ego leads us to the next spiritual goal.

Changing our Perception from Separation to Unity

The ultimate spiritual goal is to recognize the unity of all creation with the Source of creation. In my belief system, this unity is already the truth; the only thing that needs to change is my perception. The problem is that I see separation where none exists.

Objectives of Spiritual Practices

To paraphrase a quote from Einstein, the unenlightened mind cannot find enlightenment. What this means is that the mind that is engrossed in separation is not capable of perceiving unity. Achieving enlightenment is not a task to assign to the unenlightened mind. The ego cannot accomplish enlightenment nor can the ego banish the ego.

Some teachers make an enemy of the ego while other teachers acknowledge that we need the ego on the spiritual path. I do not think that our spiritual journey is enhanced by making an enemy of the ego. This view of the ego can create an unhealthy internal split and inner war that undermine our connection with peace, joy, and love. It is clear to me from my studies of various spiritual paths that the ego is with us to the end. Focusing on getting rid of the ego can be counter-productive, making the ego the center of our attention instead of focusing on the positive spiritual consciousness that we want.

At a certain point (which we will recognize when we get there), there is a move that we will be asked to make which is described as surrender, letting go, ego death, or other similar terms. In the meantime, we can prepare and move in that direction by using practices that disrupt thoughts of separation and gradually release the hold of the ego. We can also reassure ourselves that the ego will still be there until it is not there and, most of all, we do not need to worry about it.

There is a story about a disciple who wanted to find God. The guru gave the disciple a banana and instructed the disciple to go and find a place where he could be absolutely alone to eat the banana. The disciple searched far and wide but everywhere he went he felt a presence. He returned disheartened to the guru and reported that he had failed to carry out the guru's instructions to eat the banana because he couldn't find a place where he was alone. The guru declared that the disciple was enlightened.

At one point in my path, I was trying on the devotional style by connecting with a sense of longing for God as some teachers suggest. For me, this was extremely painful! I stopped doing this practice immediately. Sometime later I realized that this approach put me into the consciousness of separation from God rather than connection with God. For me, practicing the presence of my Divine Beloved and using affirmations that communicate "no separation" are much more reassuring to my heart.

"No separation" means that there is nothing that we can do and nowhere that we can go where we are separate from the Source. We can reassure ourselves that, despite appearances, we are still united with God, the Universe, or the Source of all being, using whatever language that fits your belief system.

As you put this principle into practice, you will most likely find your sense of yourself, your practice, and your relationships with others and the world expanding beyond your own individual spiritual development. As we each begin to see what unity and interconnectedness means, we will realize that what we do to others and to the planet, we are actually doing to ourselves. When we take our spiritual practices and their broader application seriously, we will be called to recognize our responsibility on a much deeper level.

5

Thoughts about Spiritual Practices

From the discussion so far, I have presented three spiritual styles and three energy levels. I have also described seven spiritual objectives. I hope from this overview that you can now see that there is no universal best practice for everyone. It all depends on your dominant style and energy level, as well as where you are in your own spiritual journey. What is right for someone else will not necessarily be right for you.

So now is the time for you to step in as your own spiritual guide and counselor. There are many possible practices to choose from. My recommendation is to start slowly and build gradually.

Finding Spiritual Practices to Choose From

I have found it worthwhile to read widely from many spiritual paths in order to get ideas and suggestions for practices that might support me. Instead of reading as a follower of a path and adopting some practice because the teacher says to do it, I read for ideas that fit what I am looking for or practices that resonate with something in me that is needing support. The test is whether I feel drawn to or connected to some practice that is described. I will try something if the practice connects with what is alive in me rather than just being something that I take on blindly because a teacher prescribes it.

Thoughts about Spiritual Practices

If reading books or listening to CDs is not your style, I have a friend who used a different strategy for getting ideas for practices. When he met someone who was more resilient and happy than he would have expected from their circumstances, he would ask them how they came to be that way. He made notes on the methods they used to overcome the challenges in their lives and to find inner peace.

I am very intentional about what I take on to do as a practice and I know why I am doing it and what I am seeking to develop in myself through the practice. I will continue doing it only as long as the practice supports my development in that area and will stop doing it when the practice has fulfilled its purpose or does not take me in the direction of my spiritual goals.

Throughout this process of finding practices, I draw from the wisdom of teachers from a broad variety of paths as well as from intuition, what I feel drawn to, and inner listening for what rings true for my own style, energy level, and issues. I am aware that what may be a good practice for some people may not be a good practice for me. I am also aware that some practices that I may want to avoid are exactly the practices that I may need, in order to overcome an obstacle in myself. I believe that developing this discernment is one of the strengths and challenges of taking responsibility for one's own spiritual path.

There are many, many sources for finding practices that already exist. I have included my own resource list in the back of this book as a possible starting place for you. Part of the fun of being your own spiritual guide is the process of attracting to you the practices that you need when you need them. Finally, if you want a practice for a specific purpose but don't have one, then go ahead and create one. Somebody created each of these practices and you can create your own too.

A Discussion of Some Practices

I want to share some thoughts about various practices which might be helpful for designing your own program, without recommending or prescribing any specific practice for you. If I have not mentioned a specific practice here, it doesn't mean that I think it is unimportant. In this section I am only discussing some practices that I believe have been misunderstood or are not usually mentioned as a spiritual practice.

About Meditation or Contemplative Practices

All meditation is not the same. There are many different forms of meditation, inner awareness, and contemplative practices and the different forms may be designed to address different spiritual objectives. For example, there are basically four possible positions for meditation: sitting, standing, walking, and lying down. Some styles of meditation may address calming the fight/flight response mechanism in the body, the autonomic nervous system. Some techniques of meditation help to create a nonjudgmental, compassionate listening space; some focus on mental awareness in the present; some focus on transcending the body. Walking meditation is designed to develop mindfulness, which is the ability to stay aware in the present moment in the midst of our activities.

Thoughts about Spiritual Practices

When choosing an awareness or meditation practice, it is important for you to ask questions about the specific technique and to understand what this style of meditation is trying to accomplish. What is the posture for? What is the breath work for? What is the chanting for? What is the mantra or repeating a specific word for?

The busy mind is normal. One purpose of meditation is to recognize this state of mind, not necessarily to change it. A problem for beginning and advanced practitioners is to think that everybody else has achieved bliss except you. I suspect that if we did a survey, and if people answered truthfully, we would find that most people have not gotten past a busy mind.

Some spiritual paths recommend meditating more regardless of the kind of difficulty a person is having. This is not necessarily good advice. I have read about a Master who advised a devotee with a dominant low energy characteristic to do "Japa Yoga," (repeating the name of God constantly) instead of meditation. I read about a Master in another path advising devotees to eat beef for a short period of time because they had overdone a practice that made them spacy and they needed some grounding. I also have read a story about the Dalai Lama changing his message in the west to emphasize compassion when he heard about the difficulty that westerners have with self-criticism and judgment in their meditations. Another example is a guru who told a disciple that she should not meditate; instead he would meditate for her.

If you want to include a meditation or contemplative practice in your spiritual program, I recommend that you examine various styles and get clarity (through wisdom, intuition, feeling, or experience) on the specific outcome that each practice is trying to accomplish. Then choose a practice that fits your spiritual needs, your spiritual style and energy level, and your lifestyle.

It is a good idea to start with short meditations and develop some consistency with your practice. Only build to longer times when you feel an inner draw to do so and end your meditation session when it is no longer enjoyable. This is not a marathon or endurance race. There is no hurry. It is better to look forward to your meditation than to dread it.

Emotional Healing

I have thankfully encountered three teachers who assert that meditation is not enough to heal emotional wounds. Meditation might be a useful support, but additional support may be needed to address emotional issues left over from childhood.

I encountered one teacher who was adamant that psychotherapy is not needed on the spiritual path. I can see a perspective that would support this point of view even though I do not agree with it. The personality can be seen, from an Eastern perspective, as a part of the illusion and, in that sense, is not real. From this perspective, achieving enlightenment will get us beyond the personality. Therefore this teacher may have believed that it is a waste of time to focus on the personality because it is an illusion.

I personally think that this viewpoint can perpetuate a lot of unnecessary suffering. Emotional trauma or wounding can be an impediment to achieving the inner peace that is needed in order to reach the enlightenment this teacher is promoting. While we are living within this illusory world, there is no need to continue to suffer emotionally if help is available.

This same teacher was quite willing to seek support from medical doctors to address physical ailments. From the Eastern perspective, the body is as much an illusion as the personality. I believe that while we are still in the illusion, we sometimes need to find the appropriate level of support for both body and emotional healing as we continue forward on the spiritual journey. We don't need to "tough it out" and continue to drag around our emotional wounds like an anchor out of some sort of spiritual purist ideals.

In my own spiritual path, I have found several useful tools to support me in healing my emotional wounds. I have the same healthy skepticism toward psychotherapists as I do towards spiritual teachers, however, I have used psychotherapists at times when I needed someone to listen to me and help me get some perspective. I have read a lot of psychotherapy books to gain some understanding of my experiences. I have also used other healing tools such as Focusing, Nonviolent Communication™, inner-child healing, Emotional Freedom Technique®, Landmark Education, Bio-Geometric Integration® chiropractic, Somatic Experiencing®, forgiveness practices, and applying feminine/masculine models to creating an intimate relationship. My suggestion is that you find the support you need to heal your emotional wounds as part of your spiritual practice.

Affirmations

Affirmations are an expression of a spiritual Truth. Repeating affirmations, whether in

Thoughts about Spiritual Practices

words or put to music in chants, is a powerful way to reprogram the subconscious mind and to keep the conscious mind busy with uplifting thoughts. Affirmations can be a powerful disrupter of the mental chatter and ego messages. During times of depression and discouragement, affirmations can be a life raft, keeping the energy moving in a positive direction.

I especially enjoy affirmations set to music because they easily circulate through the mind in the background. Have you ever tried to get an advertising jingle out of your mind? At one point, I wanted to repeat the Buddhist Loving Kindness prayer which had four lines in the version I learned. I created my own little tune to go with it and sang it to myself instead of just saying the words.

Affirmations are not the same as what is called "positive thinking." An example of positive thinking might be something like this: "Every day I feel better and better." Positive thinking has been helpful to many people, however, there is a danger of using positive thinking to mask or deny feelings that need attention and compassion.

In contrast to positive thinking, affirmations are statements of Truth from the perspective of the soul. For instance, the affirmation, "I am Joy," is true on a soul level. The power of affirmations is that they can remind us of what is true about the soul rather than focusing our attention on the conditional aspects of the world.

Humor as a Spiritual Practice

While I have never heard humor mentioned as a spiritual practice, humor is something that my husband and I use often with each other. Humor is a way of holding this world with lightness and not taking ourselves or our circumstances too seriously. Humor is a reminder to me of the illusory quality of this universe and that it is not as it appears to be. Humor reminds me that all is well even if it looks a bit odd at times. How could we miss seeing the absurdity in all that is going on in the world around us and in ourselves?

I have heard of a guru who would talk about a prank that Divine Mother had played, thus ascribing some humor even to God. Couldn't we also use humor to see beyond some of the foolishness around us? I find that being able to laugh at my own foibles helps to put a dent in the ego. When I laugh at myself, it is not so easy for the ego to stimulate feelings of shame, guilt, or embarrassment in me or to make me think I need to hide some part of myself that I might judge as unacceptable.

Manifesting as a Spiritual Practice

If you have a tendency to see yourself as a victim or to see the world as full of problems, you may want to consider some practices that help you to own your power as a divine being. From some belief systems, God is understood to be all-powerful and the creator of this universe. Further, as divine beings made in the image of God, we also are powerful co-creators of this world we see.

I believe that we have the power to manifest in this world more than we realize. I believe that we are manifesting all the time without realizing it; we are just manifesting what we <u>don't</u> want more often than what we <u>do</u> want. We can turn this around.

There are three steps to manifestation or creativity: (1) thought, (2) energy, and (3) form. First we need to have an idea or thought of what we want to create. Then we need to apply energy in that direction. Finally we need to pay attention and observe the form that manifests. The form that manifests may be something unexpected.

Somewhere, I read that we should be specific about the form we want to manifest. I do not necessarily agree. The universe is much more generous than we imagine and, I would even say, knows what we need better than we do ourselves. You have probably heard the joke about the man who is being given a tour of heaven and sees a bunch of expensive cars. He is surprised and asks what they are doing there in heaven. St. Peter replies that these were cars they tried to give to people on earth who didn't want them. The man was surprised and asked about a Cadillac. "Who wouldn't want that?" St. Peter said, "Well, in fact, this car was intended for you, but you kept praying for a

Volkswagen and that's what you got!" Given this perspective, I generally allow the details to unfold according to the design of the universe rather than get too specific.

On the other hand, I have found it helpful to identify what it is I do want and to allow myself to "dream big." Sometimes we can get stuck in believing that we don't deserve anything too good, or we are afraid of asking for too much. Maybe we will be disappointed. For me, these thoughts of limitation were left-overs from my childhood. Instead of identifying what I really wanted, I would tend to accept whatever crumbs showed up! I got the Volkswagen instead of the Cadillac!

After my divorce, I was working with myself to prepare for the kind of relationship I really wanted all along, but had instead accepted what came along. I created a list of qualities that I wanted in a partner. I had to coach myself to dream big and even make myself write down what I thought was impossible to achieve. When my future husband came into my life, I found that he had every quality I had on my list, plus more that I hadn't written down. The lesson is to dream big rather than limit what you create.

It is helpful to start manifesting in small ways in the beginning to gain some confidence in your ability to manifest. There is a joke about new disciples discovering that they are able to manifest parking places. I am not talking about manifesting parking places, although in the beginning we usually think of concrete physical things like cars and money. There is nothing wrong with manifesting physical things, but eventually we will want to apply our creativity to a higher purpose which serves others as well as ourselves.

When we become more aware of our ability to manifest, we are able to shift our consciousness from problems to solutions. For example, when we are confronted with a problem in life, the victim way of dealing with it is usually to get upset, to get depressed, to shut down or feel stuck, to complain, blame, or attack someone who we think is the cause, and to ask, "why me?" None of these victim strategies actually solve the problem but rather just create a lot of drama and suffering.

When we step into a higher level of consciousness and recognize our divine power, we shift into looking for solutions. We become calm, centered, and very practical. We ask questions like these: What is the real issue here? What needs to happen? What is absolutely perfect about this circumstance that I can work with? Is there some way that I have contributed to creating this problem in the first place? What can I do to change this situation? Am I telling myself a story about this situation that disempowers me? How can I change this story so that I am empowered to make a difference in this situation?

We get to choose whether to see ourselves as a victim or as an empowered divine being. Whichever one we choose will certainly manifest. Negative thoughts manifest as well as positive thoughts. Manifesting, as a spiritual practice, therefore, helps us to recognize our true identity as a divine being and to develop a sense of responsibility for our thoughts.

Self-Compassion

The Christian Bible tells us to love others as you love yourself. There are two parts to this directive and the first one is to love one's self. I believe it is essential that we find some way of being okay with ourselves, finding a sense of peace inside with who we are and bringing compassion and forgiveness inside.

Many of us have a hard time with this, including me. I was raised with what seemed to me as expectations for perfection as well as judgment for any short comings. I did a good job of internalizing these judgments. The result for me was an internal war – one part of me judging, fighting with, or beating up on another part of me.

What happens in most human beings is that the parts that we don't like, judge, or exile are projected out into the world around us. It is easier to judge what we don't like about ourselves when it appears to come back at us in the form of another person, culture, race, religion, or sex. It is much easier and more comfortable to disapprove of others than to confront the unwanted parts of ourselves.

I also exiled and projected many parts of me that were labeled bad and wrong. In my case, my first husband was a person who had many challenging qualities. This worked out really well for me because I got to play the role of the "good girl" and he got to be the "bad guy." After we were divorced, I began to notice many of his bad qualities showing up in me. I was surprised and astounded! These were supposed to be his qualities, not mine. As I looked more deeply, I could see how they were there in me all along, but I was conveniently distracted by judging them in him.

There is a great deal of truth in the idea that much of the violence in the world is produced by projecting what we don't like about ourselves out onto others. How can this be so? Let's break it down piece by piece.

If we start with the concept of unity, then God and all of creation is one. Everything reflected in this creation is contained in God. The duality that we see in the world is unified in God. As beings who are created in the image of God, it follows that duality is also unified in us. So both generosity and stinginess, love and hate, peace and violence can be found unified in each of us. Now when one half of a duality is identified as "good" and the other as "bad", then we human beings try to get rid of the bad part.

Growing up as children, we learn that part of us is good and part is bad, and we can gain approval from our parents if we hide or get rid of the part that is bad. Now we can't really get rid of any part of us because we are whole beings. So what we do is to project the bad part out there. So we have learned to present the "good" parts of ourselves to earn love, and to deny and project the "bad" parts of ourselves. All these "bad" parts of ourselves come back to us through other people.

When we judge or hate others, we do this without realizing that it is our own self that we are judging. Therefore, in order to love our self, we must first bring compassion to the parts of our self that we have exiled and judged as unlovable. In this way we become whole again. Then we will be able to bring compassion to others as well.

You may need to consider doing personal work that is sometimes referred to as "reclaiming our shadow." This inner work is very important for spiritual seekers especially because we are trying so hard to be good! However, the road to wholeness may require taking a trip to the dark side and reclaiming the parts of us that we have denied, exiled, and projected out onto others. Here again, a great deal of self-compassion is needed as well as appropriate support from others.

It is not hard to discover what those exiled or shadow parts are. Just look around you at the people in your life and see what they do that annoys, disgusts, angers, or upsets you. You can usually find something in yourself that is similar to that quality. There is a saying, "Change yourself, and the world changes." The secret to understanding this saying lies in understanding projection, reclaiming our shadow, and bringing love to that in ourselves that we have judged to be unlovable. Then we will no longer need to project the "bad" parts out onto the world.

I do want to acknowledge an interesting addition to this discussion of projection. Sometimes we also project out some part of us that is "good." For those people who have a low self-image or who may have taken on a role of being the weak, crazy, or bad one in their family of origin, they may have denied, exiled, and projected outward the "good" part of themselves. In this case, idealizing the high spiritual state of a guru, teacher, or fellow disciple may be projecting their own goodness onto someone else. This, too, needs to be reclaimed.

Identifying Your Needs

Identifying what you need may be a useful practice on your spiritual path. Common human needs include support, acknowledgement, intimacy, community, acceptance, freedom of choice, fun and play, consideration, meaning and purpose, trust, safety, to be heard, respect, mutuality, opportunity to contribute, and creativity. When we are able to identify what we need, then we are more empowered to find ways to meet our needs and to make clear requests of the people who support us in our life. We are less likely to be manipulative or demanding when we take charge of meeting our needs in a way that also allows the needs of others around us to be met.

Being "spiritual" does not mean that we deny our own needs in favor of other people's needs. We can become skillful in creating strategies where everyone's needs can be met. When we operate from a belief system of unity, then we have a framework for giving importance to everyone's needs getting met, including our own.

6

Finding Spiritual Fellowship

Even though you have taken responsibility for being your own spiritual guide, it may still be possible for you to find a spiritual fellowship that offers support, companionship, and a positive environment for your spiritual development. When you have identified your basic spiritual practices, you could also make a list of the qualities that you would enjoy in a spiritual community, church, or practice group. You might even want to use finding a spiritual fellowship as a project for applying the principles of manifesting discussed above.

When you have taken responsibility for your own spiritual development, connecting with a spiritual fellowship takes on a different purpose. Instead of looking to the spiritual fellowship for what to believe and prescriptions for practice, you are choosing a fellowship that will support you in the choices you have already made for yourself. You will have greater clarity about what will and will not be supportive.

Human beings develop best in connection with other human beings, so some spiritual community will likely be important for your spiritual development. Interactions with others provide us with the material we need to see ourselves better, show us areas where we need more understanding, give us opportunities to practice forgiving ourselves and others, and provide opportunities to give and receive support. No spiritual fellowship will be perfect however good a match we find, so there will always be plenty of opportunity to practice the spiritual qualities that we are trying to remember.

Spiritual fellowship helps us to strengthen our own practices just by being with people who are also following a spiritual path. I am reminded of two quotes here. First, Paramhansa Yogananda said that the environment is stronger than the will. When we surround ourselves with people who are living toward spiritual values and consciousness, it is easier for us to do the same rather than trying to fight against a current heading in the opposite direction.

Second, in the Christian Bible, Jesus is quoted as saying, "For where two or three gather in my name, there am I with them." There is power in joining with others to call on Spirit together. I recently attended a Quaker meeting for the first time and enjoyed their quiet approach to listening for Spirit together. I found their simplicity and absence of dogma to be very welcoming. I was told that many people who attend Quaker meetings come from other paths and even simultaneously follow both. This is an example of a spiritual fellowship that is open to and supports many different approaches to Spirit. There may be other spiritual fellowships that you can find that will feel welcoming to you.

Another form of spiritual fellowship may be found in a person whom you trust to provide you with empathy, compassion, honest feedback, and even validation along your journey. It is important to have someone who can listen to you when you are struggling with fears and doubts or other challenges on the spiritual path, without trying to fix it for you or offer you unsolicited advice. You might be able to find someone who would also enjoy the same kind of listening from you.

7

When You Fall into a Hole

The spiritual journey is seldom a straight line forward. In the beginning, many people experience great highs of peace, bliss, or ecstasy. They may believe that this state is the result of turning to spiritual practices. This, after all, is what they were looking for! It is working! And then there is a fall. What happened?

This pattern is so common that it must be part of the design somehow. We bring long established habits of being and thinking with us into the spiritual journey that are not overcome overnight. It is called a journey for good reason. Periods of peaks, valleys, and flats are normal. The peaks are pretty easy to be with;

the challenge is how to be with the flats and valleys.

When you are in a valley or a hole you won't necessarily recognize it right away. Most likely, you will just feel bad. When you are in a hole you will probably not have access to your resources. By definition, your consciousness has dropped, so everything will look dark. You probably won't be able to remember anything uplifting, or even want to. You won't remember why you want to be on the spiritual path in the first place. It will all look hopeless and pointless. From my experience, that's what a hole looks like from inside the hole.

The good news is that there is nothing wrong with you if you find that your spiritual journey has gone flat or that you have fallen into a hole. As your own spiritual guide, it is important that you find ways to work with yourself when this happens. Here are some ideas for you to work with as you discover through your own experience what will be helpful for you.

Understanding the Process

There is a poem that describes the experience of falling into a hole so concisely that I want to go through it here in detail. The poem is called "Autobiography in 5 Short Chapters" by Portia Nelson. You can find the short poem online at various locations, but for copyright purposes, it is not re-printed here. You can also get the point of the poem, without reading it, just from the following commentary.

Let's look at the sequence of what happens that is described in this poem. Notice that the first three chapters talk about falling into the hole. There are two things that change from chapter 1 to chapter 3. One is the amount of time that is spent in the hole, from "forever", to getting out "immediately". The second thing that changes is what the person does while in the hole.

Let's break it down, step by step:

- In chapter 1, the person is lost and helpless. In the beginning, it is difficult to know what happened, where one is, and to feel any empowerment to do anything about it. There is no access to tools or perspective, no vision of what to do. The hole is all-consuming.

- Chapter 2 is different. There is some recognition that there is a hole, but the person pretends that the hole is not there. Once he falls into the hole, this time he knows where he is and recognizes that he has been there before.

When You Fall into a Hole

- In both chapters 1 and 2, the person denies any responsibility for falling into the hole. "It is not my fault."

- In both chapters 1 and 2 it takes a long time to get out of the hole.

- Chapter 3 is a turning point. The person sees the hole and does not deny that it is there; she sees herself falling into the hole but the habit pattern is so ingrained she can't prevent it. She knows where she is; her "eyes are wide open." This time she is able to recognize her responsibility for falling into the hole. Taking responsibility, she is able to get right out again.

- In chapter 4 the person sees the hole and he does not fall in; he is able to walk around it.

- Finally in chapter 5 the person is able to anticipate the hole before it even appears and to choose to take a different path altogether.

So the steps are 1) falling into the hole, blind, helpless, and lost, 2) beginning to see and recognizing what happened after the fact, but denying responsibility, 3) taking responsibility and able to get out immediately, 4) avoiding the hole, and 5) choosing a different path. We probably spend most of our time (possibly many lifetimes) in steps 1 and 2 recycling and getting stuck in old patterns. In those stages, what can we do to help ourselves when we are in a hole?

What to Do While You are in a Hole

There is a lot of advice that is so, so easy to give when one is not in a hole or when one has progressed to stages 3-5 and is so very, very difficult to hear and implement when one is still in the first two stages. The first two stages feel like drowning in quicksand and grasping at wisps of grass on the edges as one goes down under. Nevertheless, I can't help but give some pointers on what to look for.

First of all, as soon as you can find it, bring yourself a lot of compassion. One of the hardest aspects of falling in a hole is all the judgment that we may pile on our self and the shame that we may feel for falling into a hole. In whatever way that you can, let yourself know that there is nothing wrong with you. Falling into holes is a normal part of the journey. Many saints talk about their experience wrestling with demons, which sounds to me a lot like the experience of being in a hole.

Maybe it would help to think of it like a baby who is learning how to walk for the first time.

The baby spends a lot of time falling down and struggling to get up again. That is how it strengthens its legs and learns to keep its balance. Perhaps the lesson for us is eventually learning to keep our balance by repeatedly falling into a hole.

Sometimes all you can do when you fall into a hole is hold on and wait for it to pass without scaring yourself any more than you can help it. That means to try to interrupt the self-talk, the stories that you tell yourself about what is going on (e.g., I must be going crazy; this will never end; what is wrong with me; I am so stupid; I can't survive this; I am all alone and no one cares). Reading a children's book that simplifies the problems of life can be helpful. Sometimes it might help to tell yourself, "This too shall pass." Or, if you are an active type, you might do a strenuous physical workout. If

When You Fall into a Hole

you can't do any of that, then go ahead and take a nap!

As soon as you can, find a way to allow yourself to be in the hole. Can you find a way to welcome whatever is going on and allow it space to be there? Can you avoid the inner battle with something that is telling you that you shouldn't feel this way? What ways do you know to soothe and comfort yourself? Maybe you can look around and ask with curiosity, "What happens in a hole?" Can you just listen to your self-talk, feel your energy, watch your actions, and observe what is going on? Instead of resisting the experience of being in a hole, can you dive into the experience and let it be there fully?

If you are able to go into the experience of being in a hole, maybe you can ask yourself if there is some need of yours that is not being met by what is going on in your life. Maybe something in you is trying to get your attention and give you a message about how your life is right now. Maybe there is another part of you that is afraid to hear this message, afraid of what it might have to do if it heard this message. Can you listen to both sides impartially to just hear what they have to say? If this produces too much distress at the moment, you can gently go back to your methods of soothing and calming yourself and come back to it later.

When you are feeling a bit stronger, you might be able to take a look at what happened just before you fell into the hole. Was there a triggering event? Did someone say or do something that prompted your fall? What does this remind you of from your past, from your childhood? What did you say to yourself about yourself before or while you were falling into the hole?

When You Fall into a Hole

When I am in a hole, my mind tries desperately to find a way out but usually, for some period of time, nothing I try solves the problem. From inside the hole, I lose perspective and it can feel like being in a pinball game where I am bounced from pin to pin to pin with no exit.

Underneath this, something in me believes that there actually is a solution and an inner knowing that the strategies that the hole-bound mind comes up with are not the solution. I find it interesting that even in the bottom of the hole, this inner knowing exists even if it hasn't yet fully broken through. Once it does break through the hole-bound mind, I am instantly released from the hole. So what does this liberating solution look like and how to find it more quickly without going through the pinball routine? That of course is the central issue from within the hole.

The liberating solution has a very different felt sense to it than the myriad of hole-bound solutions. I feel a sense of easing inside, an inner spaciousness, and a sense of fit. A deep breath often comes. There is a sense of recognition that the quality of this liberating solution is very different from the other solutions. The hole-bound solutions really don't offer anything that gets me out of the hole; it just feels like they bounce me to the next pin. The liberating solution feels like it evaporates the entire problem; the hole itself vanishes. So I am easily able to recognize the hole-bound solution that keeps me stuck and the liberating solution that gets me instantly out of the hole. What is not so easy is finding the liberating solution.

When I am in the hole thrashing about, I try to find self-compassion, to ask for guidance, to listen for what is needed, to get positive input from music, poetry, reading scripture, an empathy buddy, listening to an inspired teacher, affirmations, chanting, physical activity, or other form of self-care. If you find yourself frequently in a hole, you might write a letter to yourself when you are not in a hole about what you wish you could remember when you are in a hole. Then read it to yourself when you are in a hole. Don't be surprised, though, if it makes no sense to you when you are in a hole. I used to write out on the back of old business cards inspiring quotations of what I wanted to remember when I am in a hole. Then I would read these cards to myself when I was in a hole to help me remember. Sometimes these quotes gave me a wisp of grass to hold on to.

I do these kinds of things when I am in a hole, not so much because doing these things brings the liberating solution. It is more a way of keeping myself company while I am in a hole while waiting for the liberating solution to come of itself. It feels to me more like a mystical experience or grace when the liberating solution comes, rather than as a result of the things that I do while in a hole. But doing these things helps me to soothe myself and fits my active energy level.

What to Do between Holes

One key to getting out of a hole is recognizing and remembering that we are responsible for being in the hole. Taking responsibility is not the same as blaming and judging our self. Taking responsibility is something like saying the magic words "Open Sesame" to open the locked door. Taking responsibility is a magic key that changes the consciousness and provides us with access to our tools.

Taking responsibility also empowers us to notice what triggers us to fall into a hole. This step makes it more likely that we will be able to catch our self before falling in and to step around the hole the next time. This step points to work that we can do when we are not in a hole.

The time to do our emotional healing work is between holes. In between holes we have access to our resources. In between holes, we can strengthen ourselves by doing our spiritual practices. As we strengthen ourselves through our spiritual practice we will most likely find that we don't fall into holes as frequently. With practice stepping around the hole, we recognize more and more our empowerment to make choices. We have the opportunity to realize that we have even more choice than just avoiding the hole. We become empowered to choose a completely different street altogether.

8

Some Cautions

There are some good reasons why it is recommended for spiritual seekers to have a teacher and guide who has already walked the path ahead of you, who understands the pitfalls, and who knows strategies that will lead to success. I believe that the biggest obstacle to being one's own spiritual guide is that the ego will tend to run the show without our realizing it.

Of course it will! That's what the ego does and we can't stop it from trying to run the show. For me, that is not a reason to be afraid to take responsibility but rather a caution that needs to be addressed. I believe that learning to recognize the ego and call it out is a helpful spiritual practice in itself.

Here are some ways to recognize the ego.

1. You are feeling depressed, inadequate, not good enough, not perfect enough.

2. You are impatient for results, comparing yourself against saints and others who are advanced spiritual seekers.

3. You are comparing yourself against people of other paths or non-seekers and finding yourself to be more advanced and think that your path is better than theirs.

4. You focus on doing the techniques perfectly.

5. You take on more and more practices— more than you can do well.

6. You meditate for longer than you enjoy in order to rack up more hours.

7. You avoid practices that sound too confronting (but you suspect would be right for your development).

8. You jump around from practice to practice without giving any of them time and commitment.

9. You find excuses not to do your practices or make promises to yourself that you don't keep.

10. You judge yourself and beat yourself up when any of these signs shows up.

Being realistic, on a good day you may recognize only one or two of these. So what do you do when you recognize any of these signs? What I have learned to do, and sometimes even remember to do, is to forgive myself and then keep going; keep moving on even in the face of ego hijacks. I identify any of these signs as simply the ego talking and I give it to God. The ego would like nothing more than for you to give up on your spiritual practices altogether by creating discouragement or confusion.

As your own spiritual guide, there is no intermediary; no one between you and Spirit. It is up to you to monitor your progress and make adjustments to your practice; to pick yourself up when you fall and encourage yourself when you lose hope. Part of taking responsibility for your spiritual path is to do these things for yourself—but not alone. We can ask for and receive divine help. It is important for you to develop your own direct relationship with the divine however you conceive of it.

Cultivating your relationship with the divine is a key practice on the spiritual path. It is important to do this in a way that matches your concept of the divine. Prayer, or talking to a divine being, is one practice for cultivating this relationship. For some people this will be easier if the divine is personified in a human form such as Divine Mother, Jesus, Krishna, Allah, Jehovah, Buddha, the Dalai Lama, the Pope, or other human form that inspires you. For other people, some formless aspect or quality of the divine will be more inspiring such as Aum, Spirit, Love, Joy, Peace, Wisdom, Beauty, or Ground of Being.

Develop your own intuition, ask for guidance, and listen for a response. With practice, the difference between an ego response and an inspired response is usually fairly clear. Keep listening.

Another caution, whether you are launching out on your own or following a spiritual teacher, is to notice when you segment your life into spiritual and non-spiritual aspects. In my belief system, everything is spiritual. I approach all aspects of my life as part of my spiritual path including work, relationships, money, hobbies, retirement, play, communication, sexuality, food, body, emotions, needs, actions, intentions, thoughts, desires, church, school, faults, talents, illness, and anything I have forgotten to mention. Everything. There is no part of my life that I separate as being outside of God. If any part of my life is out of balance, that impacts who I am being in the world and becomes a focus of my spiritual practice.

I believe it is important not to pit one aspect of my life against another or think that I must deny some aspect of life in order to be "spiritual." There is a temptation on the spiritual path to take on a false identity that creates a shrunken caricature of human life. In my belief system, a healthy spirituality embraces all that shows up. Through my spiritual practices, I am more able to be open to life, to say "Yes!" to life, to be more fully myself, to be more present to my vitality and aliveness as the expression of God through me.

Whatever is cut off, denied, scared, hidden, out of balance, numb, or not full of life is what needs to be brought into the light through practices on your spiritual path. This takes self-awareness and most of all courage to face what may be difficult to face. When something like this comes to your attention, you may want to find some support to help you be honest and authentic with yourself. Without this objective support, there may be a tendency to use meditation and other spiritual practices as a way to avoid dealing with uncomfortable feelings and difficulties of life.

It can be easy to fool one's self into believing that it is not necessary to address these uncomfortable areas of life and that it will all evaporate through meditation. The language that is often used in the descriptions of many spiritual techniques and spiritual paths can easily feed confusion about this. I call it false advertising. The way to deal with these challenges is to go through them with self-compassion, not avoid them.

9

Measuring Progress

It is a useful practice to check in with yourself periodically to see if your spiritual practices feel more natural and are moving you directionally towards bringing you joy. Particularly when first starting out, it may take a while for a practice to feel natural. Also, if you are not feeling more joy, remember that you may be dealing with what stands between you and joy. Within this context you can ask yourself these questions as a useful test of whether your practices are supporting your spiritual development:

- Am I feeling more joy in my life?

- Do I find that I get upset less often, and things that used to bother me, don't bother me so much now?

- Do I find I am more accepting of myself and others?

If the answer is "Yes" to each of these, then you can be reassured that you are on the right track. Otherwise you might want to review what is going on in your life and determine if you need to add, subtract, or change your practices.

This review process is not an invitation to beat up on yourself or make yourself wrong for falling short. The purpose of the review is not to measure yourself but rather to see if the spiritual practices that you are doing are helpful and adequate. This periodic review gives you an opportunity to make changes as you become aware of a need to do so. Remember to bring a lot of self-compassion whenever you do a review.

As a more comprehensive check, you might also want to use the list of seven outcomes from Chapter 4 to see where you are experiencing some of what you set out to do with your spiritual practices.

1. Am I moving the energy in a positive (upward) direction?

2. Am I sometimes able to quiet the mind of the noise of self-talk?

3. Am I cultivating the Inner Witness and able to be more aware of my thoughts?

4. Do I notice that I am sometimes able to shift from fearful thoughts to loving thoughts?

5. Am I noticing more inner peace, joy, and love?

6. Am I able to be more aware of what I identify myself with and sometimes able to expand my self-identification?

7. Is my perception of this world shifting from separation to a sense of inter-connection?

Remember that spiritual development is a lifelong process. It cannot be measured by speed, but rather by small baby steps. Sometimes in the beginning, you may experience great leaps forward and then hit a plateau. This is normal and nothing to worry about. Sri Yukteswar, an Indian guru, is quoted as saying, "Everything in the future will improve if you make a spiritual effort now." If you are pointed and moving in the right direction, that is all that is needed. The rest will take care of itself through your regular practices. As one teacher said, just keep on keeping on.

In closing here is a quote, by the Persian mystic and poet Hafiz, that captures the energy of taking charge of our own spiritual path. "We have not come here to take prisoners or to confine our wondrous spirits, but to experience ever and ever more deeply our divine courage, freedom and light!"

And then there is the sweet children's round that is so profoundly simple:

> Row, row, row your boat,
> Gently down the stream.
> Merrily, merrily, merrily, merrily,
> Life is but a dream.

May your path be full of grace, your heart be light, and your joy bubble forth abundantly.

Resources

Emotional Healing

Abrams, J. Z. C. (1991). *Meeting the Shadow: The Hidden Power of the Dark Side of Human Nature.* Los Angeles; New York: J.P. Tarcher ; Distributed by St. Martin's Press.

The author offers exploration of self and practical guidance dealing with the dark side of personality based on Jung's concept of "shadow," or the forbidden and unacceptable feelings and behaviors each of us experience.

Burns, D. D. (1980). *Feeling Good: The New Mood Therapy.* New York: Morrow.

Explains how each individual can learn to control their moods through controlling the thought processes and changing the patterns of how things are perceived.

Chögyam Trungpa. (2005). *The Sanity We Are Born With: A Buddhist Approach to Psychology.* Boston: Shambhala.

Buddhist tradition teaches that all of us are born with what Chögyam Trungpa terms "basic sanity," or inherent goodness, health, and clear perception. Helping ourselves and others to connect with this intrinsic ground of sanity and health is the subject of this collection of teachings. *The Sanity We Are Born With* describes how anyone can strengthen their mental health, and it also addresses the specific problems and needs of people in profound psychological distress. The collection includes teachings on:

- Buddhist concepts of mind, ego, and intelligence, and how these ideas can be employed in working on oneself and with others

- meditation as a way of training the mind and cultivating mindfulness

- nurturing our intrinsic health and basic sanity

- guidance for psychotherapists and health professionals

Cornell, A. W. (1996). *The Power of Focusing: A Practical Guide to Emotional Self-healing*. Oakland, CA: New Harbinger Publications.

Focusing is a gentle yet powerful skill that lets you tap into your body's wisdom and make positive changes in your life. This book shows readers how they can train themselves to learn this vital technique of self-exploration and self-discovery. -- from back cover.

Gendlin, E. T. (1996). *Focusing-oriented Psychotherapy: A Manual of the Experiential Method.* New York: Guilford Press.

Examining the actual moment-to-moment process of therapy, this volume provides specific ways for therapists to engender effective movement, particularly in those difficult times when nothing seems to be happening. The book concentrates on the ongoing client therapist relationship and ways in which the therapist's responses can stimulate and enable a client's capacity for direct experiencing and "focusing." Throughout, the client therapist relationship is emphasized, both as a constant factor and in terms of how the quality of the relationship is manifested at specific times. The author also shows how certain relational responses can turn some difficulties into moments of transformative therapy.

Hendrix, H. (1988). *Getting the Love You Want: A Guide for Couples.* New York: H. Holt.

Teaches relationship skills through a ten-week home course in marital therapy.

Huber, C. (1995). *The Fear Book: Facing Fear Once and for All*. Mountain View, CA: Keep It Simple Books.

> Rather than explaining typical strategies for overcoming fear, this book focuses on examining how fear is experienced, how to recognize that experience as nothing more than conditioned reaction to circumstance, and how to mentor oneself into letting go of beliefs about "appropriate" responses to fear. The notion is debunked that fear is anything other than a label we have learned to put on a set of physical and emotional responses, which is a Buddhist view of emotion in general.

Huber, C. (2000). *Suffering is Optional: Three Keys to Freedom and Joy*. Murphys, CA: Keep It Simple Books.

> This book centers around three basic aspects of Zen practice: pay attention, believe nothing, and don't take anything personally. As ending suffering requires that one sees how suffering happens, the book urges readers to be willing to be quiet and pay attention to the process of suffering in effort to see each moment as an opportunity to step beyond illusion into freedom. It also argues that examining beliefs, abandoning them, and returning attention to the present is essential to ending suffering, as

is living in the awareness that nothing in the universe is personal.

Huber, C., & Shiver, J. (2001). There is Nothing Wrong with You: Regardless of What You Were Taught to Believe. Murphys, CA: Keep It Simple Books.

This book reveals the origin of self-hate, how self-hate works, how to identify it, and how to go beyond it. It provides examples of some of the forms self-hate takes, including taking blame but not credit, holding grudges, and trying to be perfect, and explores the many facets of self-hate, including its role in addiction, the battering cycle, and the illusion of control. After addressing these factors, it illustrates how a meditation practice can be developed and practiced in efforts to free oneself from self-hating beliefs.

May, G. G. (2005). Addiction and Grace: Love and Spirituality in the Healing of Addictions. San Francisco, CA: HarperOne.

"Drawing on his experience as a psychiatrist working with the chemically dependent, May emphasizes how addiction represents a doomed attempt to assert complete control over our lives. 'Addiction & Grace' is a compassionate and wise treatment of this important topic, offering a critical yet hopeful guide to a place of freedom based on contemplative spirituality. This 'Plus' edition includes two additional essays by Gerald May not included in the hardcover version" --Cover, p. 4.

Miller, A. (2001). *The Truth Will Set You Free: Overcoming Emotional Blindness and Finding Your True Adult Self.* New York: Basic Books.

Explores the fallout from child abuse and shares insights into how people can heal their psychic wounds from childhood.

Real, T. (1997). *I Don't Want to Talk About it: Overcoming the Secret Legacy of Male Depression.* New York: Scribner.

A study of the hidden epidemic of male depression draws on case studies to examine the causes of the ailment and how men can heal themselves, repair relationships, and break the chain of depression.

Rosenberg, M. B. (2003). *Non-violent Communication: A Language of Life: Create Your Life, Your Relationships & Your World in Harmony with Your Values.* Encinitas, CA: Puddle Dancer; Gazelle.

Do you hunger for skills to improve the quality of your relationships, to deepen your sense of personal empowerment or to simply communicate more effectively? Unfortunately, for centuries our culture has taught us to think and speak in ways that can actually perpetuate conflict, internal pain and even violence. Nonviolent Communication partners practical skills with a powerful consciousness and vocabulary to help you get what you want peacefully.

In this internationally acclaimed text, Marshall Rosenberg offers insightful stories, anecdotes, practical exercises and role-plays that will dramatically change your approach to communication for the better. Discover how the language you use can strengthen your relationships, build trust, prevent conflicts and heal pain. Revolutionary, yet simple, Nonviolent Communication offers you the most effective tools to reduce violence and create peace in your life—one interaction at a time.

Zukav, G., & Francis, L. (2002). *The Heart of the Soul: Emotional Awareness.* New York: Simon & Schuster Source.

Explains how to incorporate the principles and practices of human emotion to create a greater emotional awareness and to use emotions to develop authentic power in one's life.

Inner-Child Healing

Bradshaw, J. (1992). *Homecoming*. New York: Bantam Audio.

John Bradshaw lectures on his concept of reclaiming and championing the inner child.

Bradshaw, J. (1996). *Bradshaw on the Family a New Way of Creating Solid Self-esteem*.

John Bradshaw's seminal work on the dynamics of families that has sold more than a million copies since its original publication in 1988. Within its pages, you will discover the cause of emotionally impaired families. You will learn how unhealthy rules of behavior are passed down from parents to children, and the destructive effect this process has on our society.

Using the latest family research and recovery material in this new edition, Bradshaw also explores the individual in both a family and societal setting. He shows you ways to escape the tyranny of family-reinforced behavior traps-- from addiction and co-dependency to loss of will and denial--and demonstrates how to make conscious choices that will transform your life and the lives of your loved ones. He helps you heal yourself and then, using what you have learned helps you heal your family.

Finally, Bradshaw extends this idea to our society: by returning yourself and your family to emotional health, you can heal the world in which you live. He helps you reenvision societal conflicts from the perspective of a global family, and shares with you the power of deep democracy: how the choices you make every day can affect--and improve--your world.

Capacchione, L. (1991). *Recovery of Your Inner Child*. New York: Simon & Schuster.

The Inner Child lives within all of us, it's the part of us that feels emotions and is playful intuitive and creative. Usually hidden under our grown-up personas, the Inner Child holds the key to intimacy in relationships physical and emotional well-being, recovery from addictions, and the creativity and wisdom of our inner selves.

Recovery of Your Inner Child is the only book that shows you how to have a firsthand experience of your Inner Child -- actually feeling its emotions and recapturing its sense of wonder -- by writing and drawing with your non-dominant hand. Expanding on the highly acclaimed technique introduced in The Power of Your Other Hand, here Dr. Capacchione shares scores of hands-on activities that will help you to embrace your Vulnerable Child and your Angry Child, find the Nurturing Parent within, and finally discover the Creative and Magical Child that can heal your life.

Hendrix, H., & Hunt, H. (1997). *Giving the Love that Heals: A Guide for Parents*. New York: Pocket Books.

Explains how parents can develop a deeper, more loving relationship with their children and discusses how a person's parenting style is a reflection of the way their parents raised them, how parents can help their children choose a life partner, how parents can deal with tragedies, how parents can nurture their children, and other related topics.

Miller, A. (1997). *The Drama of the Gifted Child: The Search for the True Self* (R. Ward, Trans.). New York: BasicBooks.

Why are many of the most successful people plagued by feelings of emptiness and alienation? This wise and profound book has provided thousands of readers with an answer -- and has helped them to apply it to their own lives. Far too many of us had to learn as children to hide our own feelings, needs, and memories skillfully in order to meet our parents' expectations and win their "love." Alice Miller writes, "When I used the word 'gifted' in the title, I had in mind neither children who receive high grades in school nor children talented in a special way. I simply meant all of us who have survived an abusive childhood thanks to an ability to adapt even to unspeakable cruelty by becoming numb... Without this 'gift' offered us by nature, we would not have survived." But merely surviving is not enough. The Drama of the Gifted Child helps us to reclaim our life by discovering our own crucial needs and our own truth. -- Back cover.

Real, T. (1997). *I Don't Want to Talk About it: Overcoming the Secret Legacy of Male Depression*. New York: Scribner.

A study of the hidden epidemic of male depression draws on case studies to examine the causes of the ailment and how men can heal themselves, repair relationships, and break the chain of depression.

Whitfield, C. L. (1987). *Healing the Child Within: Discovery and Recovery for Adult Children of Dysfunctional Families*. Pompano Beach, FL: Health Communications.

Describes how the inner child is denied as a result of early trauma and loss, and how by recovering it we can heal the fear, confusion, and unhappiness of adult life.

Practices

Brother Lawrence. (1958). *The Practice of the Presence of God, Being Conversations and Letters of Nicholas Herman of Lorraine, Brother Lawrence.* Westwood, N.J.: Revell.

Inspirational classic written by a lay Carmelite Brother who served his fellow monks from the monastery kitchen.

Chödrön, P. (1997). *When Things Fall Apart: Heart Advice for Difficult Times.* Boston: Shambhala : Distributed in the United States by Random House.

Describes a traditional Buddhist approach to suffering and how embracing the painful situation and using communication, negative habits, and challenging experiences leads to emotional growth and happiness.

Chödrön, P. (2002). *Comfortable with Uncertainty: 108 Teachings.* Boston: Shambhala.

A collection of concepts and practices that teaches practical methods for heightening awareness and overcoming habitual patterns that block compassion.

Chödrön, P. (2008). *Start Where You are a Guide to Compassionate Living*: Shambhala Audio: Distributed by Random House.

Written for a modern audience, Pema Chodron gives realistic instruction on how to use an ancient Buddhist technique based in 59 slogans to find inner compassion through releasing the fear of our flaws.

Cornell, A. W. (1996). *The Power of Focusing: A Practical Guide to Emotional Self-healing*. Oakland, CA: New Harbinger Publications.

Focusing is a gentle yet powerful skill that lets you tap into your body's wisdom and make positive changes in your life. This book shows readers how they can train themselves to learn this vital technique of self-exploration and self-discovery. -- from back cover.

Cornell, A. W., & McGavin, B. (2005). *The Radical Acceptance of Everything: Living a Focusing Life*. Berkeley, CA: Calluna Press.

How can we bring peace to the inner wars that are in the way of having the life we want? For more than 30 years now, Ann Weiser Cornell has been exploring, teaching, and writing about the mysteries of emotional process, including the paradox of how we become more whole by acknowledging our parts, how the most despised places in us contain our greatest treasure, and how the body's felt sense, held in a compassionate state of Presence, is the key to change. Now her key writings have been brought together in one place, freshly edited for this volume, with four new articles offering Ann's leading-edge work. All are accessible both to the seeker of personal change and to the professional who wants to be more effective working with others.

Dalai Lama. (2002). *How to Practice: The Way to a Meaningful Life*. New York: Pocket Books.

An instructional resource and inspirational guide to daily life describes each step on the path to spiritual enlightenment and explains how to practice everyday morality, meditation, wisdom, and compassion.

Emmanuel, Rodegast, P., & Stanton, J. (1987). *Emmanuel's Book: A Manual for Living Comfortably in the Cosmos*. Toronto; New York: Bantam Books.

Here is the revealing underground classic, a delightful and invaluable guide to our inner spirit and our outer world. Emmanuel speaks to us through Pat Rodegast and shares his wisdom and insights on all aspects of life. Beautifully written and illustrated, Emmanuel's Book I is to be treasured, enjoyed and passed on to a friend. Emmanuel says: "The gifts I wish to give you are my deepest love, the safety of truth, the wisdom of the universe and the reality of God . . . . The issue of whether there is a

Greater Reality or not, for me at least, has been settled. I know that there is. So I will speak to you from the knowing that I possess." As Emmanuel points out, 'Who you are is a necessary step to being who you will be.'"

Foundation for Inner Peace. (1992). *A Course in Miracles: Combined Volume*. Glen Elen, CA: Foundation for Inner Peace.

Offers ecumenical meditations on love, perception, forgiveness, eternal life, and theoretical concepts in theology.

Huber, C. (2000). *Suffering is Optional: Three Keys to Freedom and Joy*. Murphys, CA: Keep It Simple Books.

This book centers around three basic aspects of Zen practice: pay attention, believe nothing, and don't take anything personally. As ending suffering requires that one sees how suffering happens, the book urges readers to be willing to be quiet and pay attention to the process of suffering in effort to see each moment as an opportunity to step beyond illusion into freedom. It also argues that examining beliefs, abandoning them, and returning attention to the present is essential to ending suffering, as is living in the awareness that nothing in the universe is personal.

Huber, C. (2003). *When You're Falling, Dive: Acceptance, Freedom and Possibility.* Murphys, CA: Keep It Simple Books.

This book combines the psychological concept of acceptance with ancient Buddhist teachings about the chain of interdependent origination, which provides immediately usable tools for looking at how suffering happens and how to let that go. Stressing the theme of accepting what life brings, it reveals what acceptance is and what stands in the way of being able to accept life's ups and downs. Four steps for combating resistance are also provided.

Keyes, K. (1975). *Handbook to Higher Consciousness.* Berkeley, CA: Living Love Center.

This perennial bestseller is more popular than ever and has helped countless people experience dramatic changes in their lives from the time they begin applying the simple, effective techniques.

Katie, B., & Mitchell, S. (2002). *Loving What Is: Four Questions that Can Change Your Life.* New York: Harmony Books.

Out of nowhere, like a fresh breeze in a marketplace crowded with advice on what to believe, comes the author and what she calls "The Work". In the midst of a normal life, she became increasingly depressed, and over a ten-year period sank further into rage, despair, and thoughts of suicide. Then one morning, she woke up in a state of absolute joy, filled with the realization of how her own suffering had ended. The freedom of that realization has never left her, and now in her book you can discover the same freedom through The Work. It is simply four questions that, when applied to a specific problem, enable you to see what is troubling you in an entirely different light. As she says, "It's not the problem that causes our suffering; it's our thinking about the problem." Contrary to popular belief, trying to let go of a painful thought never works; instead, once we have done The Work, the thought lets go of us. At that point, we can truly love what is, just as it is. This book will show you step-by-step, through clear and vivid examples, exactly how to use this revolutionary process for yourself. You'll see people do The Work with the author on a broad range of human problems, from a wife ready to leave her husband because he wants more sex, to a Manhattan worker paralyzed by fear of terrorism, to a woman suffering over a death in her family. Many people have discovered The Work's power to solve problems; in addition, they say that through The Work they experience a sense of lasting peace and find the clarity and energy to act, even in situations that had previously seemed impossible. If you continue to do The Work, you may discover, as many people have, that the questioning flows into every aspect of your life, effortlessly undoing the stressful thoughts that keep you from experiencing peace. This book offers everything you need to learn and live this remarkable process, and to find happiness as what the author calls "a lover of reality."

Kornfield, J. (1993). *A Path with Heart: A Guide Through the Perils and Promises of Spiritual Life.* New York, N.Y.: Bantam Books.

A guide to reconciling Buddhist spirituality with the American way of life addresses the challenges of spiritual living in the modern world and offers guidance for bringing a sense of the sacred to everyday experience.

Moore, T. (1992). *Care of the Soul: A Guide for Cultivating Depth and Sacredness in Everyday Life.* New York, NY: HarperCollins.

A guide that shows how to add spirituality, depth, and meaning to modern day life by nurturing the soul.

Nelsen, J. (2000). *From Here to Serenity: Four Principles for Understanding Who You Really Are.* Roseville, CA: Prima Pub.

A Treasure Map to Peace, Love, and Joy in Living

Is the chronic stress of modern life keeping you from enjoying the happiness that comes with peace of mind? Simple joy is needlessly missing from too many lives and from too many relationships. Inside, Dr. Jane Nelsen shows you how you can access inner peace, common sense, and daily inspiration by following four basic and easily applied principles:

- Free yourself from the filters of your thought system

- Understand how feelings can act as a personal compass

- Improve relationships by understanding and respecting differences

- Learn how to overcome depression, anger, or any negative feeling

This new, revised edition of the book Understanding provides a treasure map with which you can discover your natural feelings of peace, love, and joy.

Rosenberg, M. B. (2003). *Non-violent Communication: A Language of Life: Create Your Life, Your Relationships & Your World in Harmony with Your Values*. Encinitas, CA: Puddle Dancer; Gazelle.

Do you hunger for skills to improve the quality of your relationships, to deepen your sense of personal empowerment or to simply communicate more effectively? Unfortunately, for centuries our culture has taught us to think and speak in ways that can actually perpetuate conflict, internal pain and even violence. Nonviolent Communication partners practical skills with a powerful consciousness and vocabulary to help you get what you want peacefully.

In this internationally acclaimed text, Marshall Rosenberg offers insightful stories, anecdotes, practical exercises and role-plays that will dramatically change your approach to communication for the better. Discover how the language you use can strengthen your relationships, build trust, prevent conflicts and heal pain. Revolutionary, yet simple, Nonviolent Communication offers you the most effective tools to reduce violence and create peace in your life—one interaction at a time.

Schlitz, M. M., Vieten, C., & Amorok, T. (2007). *Living Deeply: The Art & Science of Transformation in Everyday Life*. Oakland, CA: New Harbinger Publications.

Living Deeply transcends any one approach by focusing on common elements of transformation across a variety of traditions, while affirming and supporting the diversity of approaches across religious, spiritual, scientific, academic, and cultural backgrounds. Each chapter in the book ends with Experiences of Transformation, exercises drawn from wisdom traditions or scientific investigations meant to enhance your direct experience of the material.

Opportunities to actively engage in your own transformation and that of our world are woven into the fabric of your everyday life. Learning more about the terrain of consciousness transformation can not only give you a map, but can help you become the cartographer of your own transformative journey. Research over the last decade at the Institute of Noetic Sciences (IONS) has systematically surveyed hundreds of people's stories of their own transformations, as well as conducting over 50 in-depth interviews with teachers and masters of the world's spiritual, religious, and transformative traditions.

No matter who you are, where you come from, or what your current path is - whether you seek to transform your life completely or simply make adjustments that will add a layer of richness and depth to your life - exploring the many ways that transformation is stimulated and sustained can hold great power. Weaving together cutting-edge science with wisdom from teachers of the world's transformative traditions this book explores how people experience deep shifts in their consciousness, and how those shifts can lead to healing and wholeness.

Research over the last decade at the Institute of Noetic Sciences has explored in depth the phenomenon by which people make significant shifts in the way they experience and view the world. Focusing in particular on positive transformations in consciousness, or those that result in improved health, well-being, and sense of meaning, purpose, and belonging, hundreds of people's stories of their own transformations were included in the research, as well as in-depth interviews with over 50 teachers and masters of the world's spiritual, religious, and transformative traditions.

Tolle, E. (1999). *The Power of Now: A Guide to Spiritual Enlightenment.* Novato, CA: New World Library.

To make the journey into The Power of Now we will need to leave our analytical mind and its false created self, the ego, behind. From the beginning of the first chapter we move rapidly into a significantly higher altitude where one breathes a lighter air, the air of the spiritual. Although the journey is challenging, Eckhart Tolle offers simple language and a question and answer format to guide us. The words themselves are the signposts.

Walsh, R. N. (1999). *Essential Spirituality: The 7 Central Practices to Awaken Heart and Mind.* New York: J. Wiley.

Exercises from the world's religions to cultivate kindness, love, joy, peace, vision, wisdom, and generosity.

Walters, J. D. (1996). *Meditation for Starters.* Nevada City, CA: Crystal Clarity.

Meditation brings balance into our lives, providing an oasis of profound rest and renewal. Doctors are prescribing it for a variety of stress-related diseases. This award-winning book offers simple but powerful guidelines for attaining inner peace. Learn to prepare the body and mind for meditation, special breathing techniques, ways to focus and let go, develop superconscious awareness, sharpen your willpower, and increase intuition and calmness.

Yogananda. (1974). *Scientific Healing Affirmations.* Los Angeles: Self Realization Fellowship.

Long before the use of affirmations was embraced in mainstream settings as diverse as hospitals, recovery programs, sports arenas, and corporate suites, the renowned mystic Paramahansa Yogananda - author of the spiritual classic Autobiography of a Yogi, - understood and taught the deep spiritual principles that make this ancient scientific tool so powerfully effective. Scientific Healing Affirmations reveals the hidden laws for harnessing the power of concentrated thought - not only for physical healing, but to overcome obstacles and create all-around success in our lives. Included are comprehensive instructions and a wide variety of affirmations for healing the body, developing confidence, awakening wisdom, curing bad habits, and much more.

Yogananda, P., & Kriyananda, S. (2011). *Ananda Chants*. Nevada City, CA: Crystal Clarity.

A collection of chants with words and music.

Relationships

Chapman, G. D. (1995). *The Five Love Languages: How to Express Heartfelt Commitment to Your Mate.* Chicago: Northfield Pub.

People express and receive love in different Ways. Dr. Chapman identifies these as the five languages of love: Quality time, Words of affirmation, Gifts, Acts of service, and Physical touch. In this new edition, you will find a couple's guide to help you work as a team and learn to speak and understand the unique languages of love.

Hendrix, H. (1988). *Getting the Love You Want: A Guide for Couples.* New York: H. Holt.

Teaches relationship skills through a ten-week home course in marital therapy.

Huber, C. (1997). *Be the Person You Want to Find: Relationship and Self-discovery.* Mountain View, CA: Keep It Simple Books.

This guide to self-discovery through intimate relationships offers a spiritual perspective on healing childhood wounds and destructive patterns that are learned early on and later cause relationship dysfunction in adulthood.

Peck, M. S. (1978). *The Road Less Traveled: A New Psychology of Love, Traditional Values, and Spiritual Growth.* New York: Simon and Schuster.

Discusses the nature of loving relationships in the context of traditional psychological and spiritual insights.

Richo, D. (2002). *How to be an Adult in Relationships: The Five Keys to Mindful Loving.* Boston: Shambhala.

Author Richo offers a fresh perspective on love and relationships--one that focuses not on finding an ideal mate, but on becoming a more loving and realistic person. Drawing on the Buddhist concept of mindfulness, he explores five hallmarks of mindful loving and how they play a key role in our relationships throughout life, helping us to move away from judgment, fear, and blame to a position of openness, compassion, and realism about life and relationships.--From publisher description.

Spirituality

Bossis, G. (1985). *He and I*. Sherbrooke, Quebec: Editions Paulines.

Enter into the intimate, interior conversations between Jesus and Gabrielle Bossis. In this timeless spiritual classic, you share in the profound and touching experience of Gabrielle Bossis-a French nurse and playwright living as a single woman in the early 20th century-while she hears the inner voice of Jesus in the core of her being.

It was not until the age of 62 while traveling to Canada aboard the 'Ile de France' that Gabrielle began a dialogue with this inner voice. From that time until two weeks before her death in 1950, the voice of Jesus summoned her not only in church and during prayer, but amidst the hustle and bustle of modern life. From flying on an airplane, to riding the metro during rush hour in Paris, to walking through the crowds of busy city streets, to performing on a theatrical stage, Gabrielle encountered Jesus during all of her experiences. Even when she was contemplating her innermost thoughts and feelings, Jesus was striking up a conversation with her.

Recorded in her diary from 1936 to 1950, their tender exchanges capture Gabrielle's transformative spiritual journey as her doubt evolves into confidence. But they also capture Jesus' enduring presence in our daily lives, his insistence on serving others with kindness, and his encompassing love for humanity-and show that you, too, can experience an intimacy with Christ.

Brach, T. (2003). *Radical Acceptance: Embracing Your Life with the Heart of a Buddha*. New York: Bantam Books.

Combining the principles of psychotherapy with the teachings of Buddhism, this guide explains how to eliminate the personal conflicts and feelings of not being good enough that can cause such problems as addiction, overwork, and perfectionism.

Emmanuel, Rodegast, P., & Stanton, J. (1987). *Emmanuel's Book: A Manual for Living Comfortably in the Cosmos*. Toronto; New York: Bantam Books.

Here is the revealing underground classic, a delightful and invaluable guide to our inner spirit and our outer world. Emmanuel speaks to us through Pat Rodegast and shares his wisdom and insights on all aspects of life. Beautifully written and illustrated, Emmanuel's Book I is to be treasured, enjoyed and passed on to a friend. Emmanuel says: "The gifts I wish to give you are my deepest love, the safety of truth, the wisdom of the universe and the reality of God . . . . The issue of whether there is a Greater Reality or not, for me at least, has been settled. I know that there is. So I will speak to you from the knowing that I possess." As Emmanuel points out, 'Who you are is a necessary step to being who you will be.'"

Foundation for Inner Peace. (1992). *A Course in Miracles: Combined Volume*. Glen Elen, CA: Foundation for Inner Peace.

Offers ecumenical meditations on love, perception, forgiveness, eternal life, and theoretical concepts in theology.

Goldstein, J., & Kornfield, J. (1988). *Seeking the Heart of Wisdom*. Shambhala.

In Seeking the Heart of Wisdom Goldstein and Kornfield present the central teachings and practices of insight meditation in a clear and personal language. The path of insight meditation is a journey of understanding our bodies, our minds, and our lives, of seeing clearly the true nature of experience. The authors guide the reader in developing the openness and compassion that are at the heart of this spiritual practice. For those already treading the path, as well as those just starting out, this book will be a welcome companion along the way. Useful exercises are presented alongside the teachings to help readers deepen their understanding of the subjects. Among the topics covered are:

- The hindrances to meditation—ranging from doubt and fear to painful knees—and skillful means of overcoming them

- How compassion can arise in response to the suffering we see in our own lives and in the world

- How to integrate a life of responsible action and service with a meditative life based on nonattachment

Hillman, J. (1996). *The Soul's Code: In Search of Character and Calling.* New York: Random House.

"Plato and the Greeks called it "daimon," the Romans "genius," the Christians "guardian angel"; today we use terms such as "heart," "spirit," and "soul." For James Hillman it is the central and guiding force of his utterly unique and compelling "acorn theory," which proposes that each life is formed by a particular image, an image that is the essence of that life and calls it to a destiny, just as the mighty oak's destiny is written in the tiny acorn. It is a theory that offers a liberating vision of childhood troubles and an exciting approach to themes such as fate and fatalism, character and desire, family influence and freedom, and, most of all, calling - that invisible mystery at the center of every life that speaks to the fundamental question "What is it, in my heart, that I must do, be, and have? And why?"" "The Soul's Code dedicates itself to what is truly innate, not to how it got this way or where it's going. Hillman does not see human beings as results or, worse, victims of their lives, nor does the promise or even seek a "cure"; instead he welcomes the necessity of every aspect of what makes up a life and advocates using "symptoms" as clues to what the daimon demands. Essentially, Hillman believes that there is more to life - to each individual - than can be explained by the traditional "either/or" categories of genetics and environment. His method is to use the extraordinary (an extensive array of examples from Yehudi Menuhin to Jeffrey Dahmer) as a way to inspire the ordinary, as well as urging his readers to reexamine their childhood impulses, fantasies, thoughts, and even accidents, all of which reflect the "blueprints" that give direction to the course of a biography."--BOOK JACKET.

Keyes, K. (1975). *Handbook to Higher Consciousness*. Berkeley, CA: Living Love Center.

This perennial bestseller is more popular than ever and has helped countless people experience dramatic changes in their lives from the time they begin applying the simple, effective techniques.

Kornfield, J. (1993). *A Path with Heart: A Guide Through the Perils and Promises of Spiritual Life*. New York, N.Y.: Bantam Books.

A guide to reconciling Buddhist spirituality with the American way of life addresses the challenges of spiritual living in the modern world and offers guidance for bringing a sense of the sacred to everyday experience.

Ram Dass. (1976). *The Only Dance There Is*. New York: J. Aronson.

This book is based on talks by Ram Dass at the Menninger Foundation in 1970 and at the Spring Grove Hospital in Maryland in 1972. The text grew out of the interaction between Ram Dass and the spiritual seekers in attendance at these talks. The result of this unique exchange is a useful guide for understanding the nature of consciousness--useful both to other spiritual seekers and to formally trained psychologists. It is also a celebration of the Dance of Life--which, in the words of Ram Dass, is the "only dance there is."

Renard, G. R. (2005). *The Disappearance of the Universe.* London: Hay House.

An uncompromising introduction to A Course in Miracles: a spiritual teaching destined to change human history.

Saint Teresa of Avila, & Peers, E. A. (1991). *The Way of Perfection.* New York: Doubleday.

St. Teresa of Avila was a prominent 16th-century Spanish mystic and Carmelite nun. This is her great work on the practice of prayer, consisting of detailed directions on the achievement of spiritual perfection. It has long been considered a classic of the interior life and Christian mysticism, and modern readers will appreciate its warmth and accessibility.

Schlitz, M. M., Vieten, C., & Amorok, T. (2007). *Living Deeply: The Art & Science of Transformation in Everyday Life.* Oakland, CA: New Harbinger Publications.

Living Deeply transcends any one approach by focusing on common elements of transformation across a variety of traditions, while affirming and supporting the diversity of approaches across religious, spiritual, scientific, academic, and cultural backgrounds. Each chapter in the book ends with Experiences of Transformation, exercises drawn from wisdom traditions or scientific investigations meant to enhance your direct experience of the material.

Opportunities to actively engage in your own transformation and that of our world are woven into the fabric of your everyday life. Learning more about the terrain of consciousness transformation can not only give you a map, but can help you become the cartographer of your own transformative journey. Research over the last decade at the Institute of Noetic Sciences (IONS) has systematically surveyed hundreds of people's stories of their own transformations, as well as conducting over 50 in-depth interviews with teachers and masters of the world's spiritual, religious, and transformative traditions.

No matter who you are, where you come from, or what your current path is - whether you seek to transform your life completely or simply make adjustments that will add a layer of richness and depth to your life - exploring the many ways that transformation is stimulated and sustained can hold great power. Weaving together cutting-edge science with wisdom from teachers of the world's transformative traditions this book explores how people experience deep shifts in their consciousness, and how those shifts can lead to healing and wholeness.

Research over the last decade at the Institute of Noetic Sciences has explored in depth the phenomenon by which people make significant shifts in the way they experience and view the world. Focusing in particular on positive transformations in consciousness, or those that result in improved health, well-being, and sense of meaning, purpose, and belonging, hundreds of people's stories of their own transformations were included in the research, as well as in-depth interviews with over 50 teachers and masters of the world's spiritual, religious, and transformative traditions.

Vanamali. (1996). *The Play of God: Visions of the Life of Krishna*. San Diego, CA: Blue Dove Press.

Just as the call of Krishna's heavenly flute is irresistibly attractive, so this book will enchant and uplift its readers. Never before has the complete life of Krishna been told in a way that is so engaging and understandable, yet so faithful to the ancient epics of India. Spiritual seekers of all traditions will find inspiration and revitalized faith in these pages.

The Play of God is the account of a spiritual phenomenon. It describes the extraordinary manifestation of the divine that was Krishna, the playful and enchantingly beautiful deity who epitomizes the highest principles of India's spiritual vision. While the usual Western image of God as father or monarch is represented in this story, readers will also find here much more -- a refreshing and powerful picture of God as child, playmate, lover, friend, and teacher. They will discover how India conceived the most intimate and joyous experience of God, using the seductive metaphor of the Divine Beloved. What is evoked here is not a religion of moral law and stern obligation, but a spirituality of joy and true desire, love and beauty, contemplation and inner awakening.

This life of Krishna expands our concept of divinity and raises our thoughts to a higher spiritual plane. What does it mean to conceive of God as warrior and king? What does it mean to relate to the Infinite as friend or husband? Such experiences are vividly portrayed in these pages. We are uplifted as we contemplate the unlimited joy of the Eternal, appearing to us in a form combining beauty, strength, and irrepressible playfulness. Just as the music from Krishna's heavenly flute is irresistibly attractive, so this book will entrance its readers. Never before has the complete life of Krishna been told in a way that is so engaging and understandable, yet so faithful to the ancient epics of India.

Walters, J. D. (1998). *The Hindu Way of Awakening: Its Revelation, its Symbol, an Essential View of Religion.* Nevada City, CA: Crystal Clarity Publishers.

This book is delightful reading for anyone interested in spirituality and the deeper meanings of religion. A master of word imagery, Swami Kriyananda brings order to the seeming chaos of symbols and deities in Hinduism. This book reveals the underlying teachings from which the symbols arise, the truths inherent in all religions, and their essential purpose the direct inner experience of God. Divided into two sections of ten chapters each, the author leads the reader to clarity as can be done only by someone who has achieved that clarity himself.

Wilber, K. (1981). *No Boundary: Eastern and Western Approaches to Personal Growth.* Boulder, CO: Shambhala.

A simple yet comprehensive guide to the types of psychologies and therapies available from Eastern and Western sources. Each chapter includes a specific exercise designed to help the reader understand the nature and practice of the specific therapies. Wilber presents an easy-to-use map of human consciousness against which the various therapies are introduced and explained.

Wilber, K. (2006). *Integral Spirituality: A Startling New Role for Religion in the Modern and Postmodern World*. Boston: Integral Books.

Integral Spirituality is being widely called the most important book on spirituality in our time. Applying his highly acclaimed integral approach, Ken Wilber formulates a theory of spirituality that honors the truths of modernity and postmodernity—including the revolutions in science and culture—while incorporating the essential insights of the great religions. He shows how spirituality today combines the enlightenment of the East, which excels at cultivating higher states of consciousness, with the enlightenment of the West, which offers developmental and psychodynamic psychology. Each contributes key components to a more integral spirituality.

On the basis of this integral framework, a radically new role for the world's religions is proposed. Because these religions have such a tremendous influence on the worldview of the majority of the earth's population, they are in a privileged position to address some of the biggest conflicts we face. By adopting a more integral view, the great religions can act as facilitators of human development: from magic to mythic to rational to pluralistic to integral—and to a global society that honors and includes all the stations of life along the way

Yogananda. (1981). *Autobiography of a Yogi.* Los Angeles: Self-Realization Fellowship.

An autobiographical account of an early nineteenth-century yogi as he reaches self-realization, identification with his larger self, mankind, and union with his God.

Harmony World Publishing

Harmony World Publishing is dedicated to facilitating the development of world peace and the advancement of human communication and relationships through publishing books, articles, blogs, and other written materials. The Japanese word for harmony, Aiki, is the ability to harmonize with an opponent's energy and is one of the essential qualities for a traditional Japanese warrior. This principle of Aiki is essential in political, business, and social leaders as well as in families, schools, and social activism. The promotion of world harmony requires strength, commitment, inner discipline, and courage. Harmony is the opposite of domination of one person, group, or idea over another. The ability to relate effectively with people of diverse cultures and perspectives is a hallmark of harmony as is the ability to find solutions through collaboration and dialogue that meet everyone's needs. There is a need in our world for increasing the skills of people at all levels to facilitate peace building activities and communication. To this end, Harmony World Publishing promotes materials that support the development of understanding and skillfulness in facilitating peace.

website: www.harmonyworld.net

Happiness is a Good Store: Finding Meaning in Life's Experiences. This book uses many personal stories and examples to describe how you can create more happiness in your life through becoming aware of your meaning-making process. Our personal stories shape our lives. Human beings were designed to create stories, make meaning, and interpret the world we perceive. This ability to make meaning defines our humanity as opposed to animals or plants. Our stories about ourselves and others are the meaning that we have made up to make sense of something that happened. However, our suffering also lies primarily in the meaning that we give to what happened. If we assign the meaning to what happened, then we also are empowered to change the meaning that we create. To regain our empowerment, we have an opportunity to create stories that open up new possibilities, "re-frame" a situation, or re-tell our story to our self from a different framework. This book provides specific examples for how to transform your meaning-making process from one that is disempowering to one that empowers you as the hero of your own story. ISBN 978-0-9911-1170-1

...the Professional Series

Empathy in Conflict Intervention: The Key to Successful NVC Mediation. The focus of this book is on mediation, a third party intervention role that can be undertaken by supervisors, managers, human resource professionals, marriage and family therapists, teachers, mediators, peace keepers, and parents. The authors make a strong case for the central role of empathy in promoting a successful mediation, especially when ongoing relationships between the parties are at stake. This book provides a thoughtful study of the important role of empathy in mediation through the development of a theoretical model to explain the effectiveness of Nonviolent Communication™ (NVC) mediation. The theory building process used in this book, as well as the list of conditions for a successful mediation, can be broadly applied to other third party intervention methods. ISBN 978-1-4776-1460-0

Available now at www.harmonyworld.net.

About the Authors

Rev. Nelle Moffett, Ph.D., was raised in the Presbyterian Church and her father was the minister. Nelle became "Spiritual but not religious" as a result of taking a college course in Oriental Mysticism. She majored in Philosophy and began a search for a framework for understanding herself and God. After 10 years, Nelle became a disciple of Paramhansa Yogananda, who came to America to show the underlying unity of original Christianity and original Yoga. Since then, Nelle has explored many spiritual teachings including various branches of Buddhism, Christian saints and mystics, Hindu teachers, *A Course in Miracles*, Inner Relationship Focusing, psychology and philosophy. Nelle is a certified Life Coach. Nelle is an ordained interfaith minister and co-founder of Common Ground Interspiritual Fellowship.
Email: moffett@cgiFellowship.org

Rev. Rick Bowers was brought up in a military family and went to non-denominational protestant churches on military bases. In his late teenage years, the interpretations taught in the Christian churches he attended generated more questions than answers and he became "Spiritual but not religious." After many years as an agnostic, Rick was introduced to the teachings of Paramhansa Yogananda and became a disciple. Rick lived in a spiritual community for several years where he met his wife, Nelle. Rick is committed to teaching communication skills to create peace in the world. Together, Rick and Nelle have a consulting company, Speak Peace, where they teach communication skills with individuals, parents, families, couples, and businesses. Rick is an ordained interfaith minister and co-founder of Common Ground Interspiritual Fellowship. Email: bowers@cgiFellowship.org

www.ingramcontent.com/pod-product-compliance
Lightning Source LLC
Chambersburg PA
CBHW061946070426
42450CB00007BA/1068